Stepping out From a Technical Job And Leaping into Management

Stepping out From a Technical Job And Leaping into Management

A Dissertation

Martin K. Younts

iUniverse, Inc.
New York Lincoln Shanghai

Stepping out From a Technical Job And Leaping into Management
A Dissertation

iUniverse books may be ordered through booksellers or by contacting:

iUniverse
2021 Pine Lake Road, Suite 100
Lincoln, NE 68512
www.iuniverse.com
1-800-Authors (1-800-288-4677)

ISBN-13: 978-0-595-39594-1 (pbk)
ISBN-13: 978-0-595-83997-1 (ebk)
ISBN-10: 0-595-39594-5 (pbk)
ISBN-10: 0-595-83997-5 (ebk)

Printed in the United States of America

Contents

List of Tables

List of Figures

Abstract

TRANSITIONING FROM A TECHNICAL COMPETENCY TO A
MANAGEMENT COMPETENCY WITHIN THE DEPARTMENT
OF DEFENSE BRANCH OF THE FEDERAL GOVERNMENT

Problem

This study will explore the challenges faced in the transition from a
technical competency to a management competency by Technical
Specialist (TS) as they moved to the position of Program Manager (PM) in
the Defense Acquisition Workforce (DAW). And to understand the up hill
challenges faced in this transition through their experiences. As most TS
move into a PM position they not only find it a difficult transition but
they must also complete a three level certification process in the Defense
Acquisition Workforce Improvement Act (DAWIA).

The Defense Acquisition Workforce Improvement Act plays a significant role and is a major part of the certification process in the federal government sector. This act attempts to find careerist having a professional
technical background such as an engineering degree and then grooming
them in a way for promotion and certification into the management field.
However, once you have become a highly competent technical specialist
the transition becomes hard to obtain as well and getting accepted into
the management competency. Therefore, a very small amount of technical specialist ends up being selected. Due to the very nature of this
research very little material was available. For the purpose of this study
the material used was as near to the subject matter that this writer could
find and that would closely fit into the subject area of study as transitions
from a technical or professional back ground to a management role in the

private sector of an organization and the skills needed in becoming a manager.

This study will examine those technical specialists who made the transition and the challenges, experiences and the individual transition into the new competency.

Method

The qualitative approach method was used to collect information via interviews, This exploratory researched was to look at the technical specialist moving into a program management position within the Federal Government Department of Defense (D.O.D) by putting emphasis on what experiences were common and challenges the individuals faced in the transitions. Interviews were conducted with five governmental PM's who successfully transitioned from TS to PM in government service and completed the DAWIA certification program.

Each interview was either by email or phone conversations. These interviews were also designed not to take more than 60 minutes and once collected they were transcribed. The program managers worked for the Department of Defense Logistics Competency at Point Mugu, California, Pax River, Maryland and China Lake, California. There were four research questions formulated to provide the basis for analyzing and presenting the results of this almost impossible transition.

Findings

The findings of this study revealed key issues or skills needed to become an effective manager. The PM's experiences were identified then grouped into areas of discussion. Once gathered these experiences and areas of discussion were presented back to the program managers who validated them and ranked them according. Four main areas of discussion were considered to be the foremost topics or aspects of the transitioning into program management.

They were:

(1) **Expectations of the new position:** The perception of the newly acquired position and the reality of the newly appointed position.

(2) **Abundance of issues:** As becoming a Program Manager their roles and responsibilities have increased enormously, with tasking and the setting of priorities more so then being a Technical Specialist.

(3) **Affiliation changes:** Since becoming a Program Manager how has your personal relationships changed and the interactions with them and other technical specialist of you changed. Have the perceptions of the technical specialist changed towards you.

(4) **Allocating:** As Program a Manager how challenging is it to leave the hands on approach and getting task accomplished through others.

Conclusion

The research of this study will show that the program managers spent three years on average in their transitional phase and in their developmental process after working in their newly appoint position. In the writer's view, this was a significant aspect of the transition, a three-year learning curve before the mangers in question felt comfortable enough and confident enough to perform their new position and to leave the technical aspect alone.

Acknowledgments

I would like to express my gratitude to my, friends and colleagues who have shared information and reviewed portions of this paper as well as offered insights and comments.

I would also like to thank my wife, Diana Cianca Younts, for her support and continuous encouragement during the final paper portion of the degree program.

Martin K. Younts

Chapter 1

Introduction

The practice of management is as old as recorded history. Throughout time people have joined together to accomplish a goal. There were fundamentally three processes of thoughts in the evolution of management the Classical, Behavioral, and the Management Science School. Classical management is considered to be a combination of classical and scientific theory. There were two individuals that can stand out for this theory, F.W. Taylor and H. Fayol, Taylor for his scientific approach and Fayol for his classical organizational theory better known as administrative theory (Donnelly, Gibson & Ivancevich, 1985, p.40). Also one other maybe not so well known Mary Parker Follet "who advocated a collaborative approach in solving problems in the work place". She was a pioneer in conflict resolution (Montana & Charnov, 2000, p.18).

Problem

The problem of this study is to discover what challenges did the TS face in their transition from a technical competency to a management competency by Technical Specialist (TS) as they moved to the position of Program Manager (PM) in the Defense Acquisition Workforce (DAW). And to understand the difficulties and challenges faced in this transition though their experiences. As most TS move into a PM position they not only find it a difficult transition but they must also complete a certification process that entails three levels and they are given eighteen months to complete. This process is in the Defense Acquisition Workforce Improvement Act (DAWIA).

1

DAWIA had the intent of capturing and transforming technical trades to the DAW of management occupations. As technical specialists tried to acquire the skills needed to enter the management competency in the DAWIA program and completing their certification process. It became an uphill challenge as they became more skilled in their trade. Similar issues as were developing between engineers and management in the private sector, Badawy (1995) indicated a new order was bought about by changes in technology; markets; global competition; education, socioeconomic ideologies and values; and a new management order requires new management technologies, policies, and leadership styles to respond, manage, and cope with the change.

The transition of technologist into management has been a known problem for years and now in the 21st century new skills have to be learned for technologist to succeed as a manager. Badawy (1995) indicated that according to a survey he administered, "about 80 percent of engineers and scientist indicated that their career goal was to become a manger within five years (p.64). Aucoin (2002) indicated that according to a survey that was administered by the Institute of Electrical and Electronics Engineers (IEEE), "approximately 70 percent of engineers indicated that they had some supervisory responsibilities" (p.3).

The education (and early on-the-job experience) of modern engineers is an intensive and demanding one. Heavy emphasis is placed on deep technical understanding and effective application of theory and experiment in the solution of engineering problems. There is little time for broader contemplation of how the technical efforts fit into the larger content or even where the challenging problems come from (Gray 1979). According to an example from Aucoin (2002), stated ultimately, an engineer is typically valued as the technical expert.

While this expertise is a worthwhile asset after the transition, a manger must quickly recognize that technical prowess is usually not the most important factor of the success for his work and that of his team. As professional occupations such as the technical specialist or an engineer both in the federal government and in the private sector they both need to acquire additional skills to fully benefit their transition.

Hill (2003) while conducting her study showed that the research she performed was just as inadequate as it was in the technologist transitioning to management when she said: "despite its ubiquity and importance we know surprisingly little about the transition to management" (Hill, 2003, p. 2). Furthermore, after the studies had been done on transitions to management and that we knew surprisingly little about how managers do their jobs" (p. 337).

Hill (2003) once stated that it appeared that the problem was that the term transition is often treated "as an event rather than a process and researchers usually ignored the more person-centered aspects of the transition" (p. 338).

Purpose of the Study

The purpose of the study was to embrace a method for determining the difficulties and skills needed to be acquired for the TS new roles as a PM and what challenges was faced by the technical specialist as they attempted to transition into the program managers role. As TS are mainly of an engineering discipline once their skills on the technical competency matured it became harder to transition into any other competency especially one in management. Their have been a very few TS promoted into the management field and this study wanted to conduct a exploratory approach with a qualitative method with a descriptive survey to show the those technical specialists who made the transition and the challenges, experiences and the individual transition into the new competency and the skills acquired that are needed with the position of program manager. There has been very little if any ever research done on this topic and none known by this writer.

Hill (2003) while conducting her study showed that the research she performed was just as inadequate as it was in the technologist transitioning to management when she said: "after the studies had been done on transitions to management and that we knew surprisingly little about how managers do their jobs" (p. 337). Hill (2003) also stated that the problem with transition in her view was often treated as an event rather than a process and researches have an inclination to ignore the person centered aspect of the transition (p. 338).

By this omission another issue claims in the literature that a transition from technologist to manager is also difficult and that there isn't research to back up these events either. This as well is closely with this study. Furthermore, the reasons for the difficulty in the transition are not clearly understood. Capturing the intent of the DAWIA occupations and professions became important factor in this research. During the first part of this century scientific and technological advances led to an ever-increasing level of diversification and specialization in the workforce.

Importance of the Study

The importance of this study focuses on trying to understand what challenges lay head for the successful transition from technical specialist to program manager with in the department of defense in the federal government. And the skills needed to acquire the position and to fully understanding the expectations required in management field. The exploratory approach method was chosen with an objective by using a qualitative method with a descriptive survey was the main focus of this study on finding the very nature of technical specialist transition to a program manager. The following questions were formulated to study and examined their transition.

1. How were their technical expertise related to a managerial related context during the transition from a TS to a PM?

2. Are the management aspects of the position more challenging then first thought, once appointed to management was there a career developmental program?

3. Were there any certifications that needed to be completed and if so what was the process like?

4. What did they like while being a TS and now as a PM, and the same for their dislikes on both positions?

5. How and if any individual and organizational resources do they rely on and were there any commonality between being a technical specialist and a program manager?

6. How difficult were and what were the main issues in the transition from TS to PM?

The questions above were designed to create an assessment from other research in literature found in management, which are transitions. In addition, to this type of questioning the term technologists came to be used as professions in technical or specialty fields. And then hence the term technologist came to be for the purpose of this study transitioning into management and the development of or the technologist. (Badawy, 1995, p.4). The questions will be talked about in the following order.

1. How were their technical expertise related to a managerial related context during the transition from a TS to a PM?

2. Are the management aspects of the position more challenging then first thought, once appointed to management was there a career developmental program?

3. Were there was any certification that needed to be completed and if so what was the process like?

4. What did they like while being a TS and now as a PM, and the same for their dislikes on both positions?

The importance of this question is to provide information for a better understanding the challenges faced in the transition.

5. How and if any individual and organizational resources do they rely on and were there any commonality between being a technical specialist and a program manager?

This question is to help identify the commonality of experiences of the TS and the PM.

6. How difficult were and what were the main issues in the transition from TS to PM?

This question it will provide insightfulness in the regard in the transition from TS to PM. A better understanding of the challenges and difficulties experienced throughout the transition is the intension of this writer to provide a necessary contribution for others that face a management transition from a specialty or professional background. It should make for a beginning of a solid foundation for any other government agency.

Scope of the Study

The study was focused on technical specialist, which held a professional degree in engineering and now holds a program manager position in the federal government of the department of defense. There locations where Pax River Maryland, Pt. Mugu California and China Lake California. Technical specialist are an important part of the technical/engineering workforce, their were only a small amount of TS in this division of the weapons group and due to locations this study was limited to only those sites or locations. These results only account for the technical specialist within the weapons branch of the department of defense and therefore, it's accuracy for other specialist within other departments in the federal government may not correspond in the other groups or locations.

Rationale of the Study

This study examined the transition from being a technical specialist within the weapons division of the D.O.D branch of the Federal Government to program manager. Each interviewee held an engineering degree, and they were situated in three locations.

The rational for this study was to get a better understanding on what the difficulties were, the challenges they faced, their expectations if any, and commonality existed between the two positions. The certification process was difficult to obtain and how long did it take them in terms of months to achieve such a certification. The researcher of this study deemed it was necessary and important to understand what each of the technical specialist personally experienced during their transition. By researching and formulating the results of those experiences it could provide priceless insight into future transitions of other TS and a better understanding of the challenges faced in the transition from being a technical specialist to becoming a program manager in the weapons branch of the department of defense. And this could lay the foundation of their experiences and would hopefully lessen the difficulty for the individual who maybe considered for the transition. From this a career development path may be established for the ability of TS who wishes to target the management career field. By researching such study it may possibly spark interest for a further study due to the findings of this data

Definition of Terms

Following are technical terms used herein.

1. Delegates: is a person authorized or sent to speak and act for others. (Webster's Third New World Dictionary, 1991, p. 364).

2. DAWIA: the Defense Acquisition Workforce Improvement Act. Was established for both the Defense Acquisition Workforce (DAW) members. The act requires that D.O.D. designate specific jobs as "Program Manager" positions and provide a structured approach for filling these designated positions. (Acquisition Career Development Program Manual. (DOD 5000.52-M).

3. DAWIA Certification: is the act of certifying by completing the mandatory experience, education, and training standards for each level. (Acquisition Career Development Program Manual. (DOD 5000.52-M)

4. Dysfunctional: Usually is emotional and involves destructive disagreements. (Management Skills, 2001, p.130)

5. Manager: Is a person working for an organization that practices management, makes decisions, solves problems, and is responsible for the work of at least one other individual reporting to him managerial work? (Developing Managerial Skills in engineers and Scientist, 1995, p. 6)

6. Management: is a process comprising several activities and tasks to be undertaken or accomplished: planning, organizing, directing, and controlling. Without undertaken these task, you are not a manager-you are a specialist, an expert, or a consultant serving in an advisory capacity. (Developing Managerial Skills in engineers and Scientist, 1995, p. 5)

7. Profession: A vocation or occupation requiring advanced education and training, and involving intellectual skills as engineering, medicine, law theology ect. (Webster's Third New World Dictionary, 1991, p 1074).

8. Program Management: Is the individual designated in accordance with criteria established by the appropriate Component Acquisition Executive to manage an acquisition program and appropriately certified under the provisions of the Defense Acquisition Workforce Improvement Act? A PM has no other command or staff responsibilities within the Component. The program manager (PM) has responsibility for one or more acquisition programs. Program management includes other positions that directly or indirectly assist the PM in fulfilling assigned responsibilities. (Acquisition Career Development Program Manual. (DOD 5000.52-M)

9. Specialist: is one who devotes him or herself to a special occupation or a branch of learning. (Webster's Third New World Dictionary, 1991, p. 874).

10. Technical skills: are skills that include the ability of the manager to develop and apply certain methods and techniques related to his task. The manager's technical skills also encompass a general familiarity with and understanding of the technical activities undertaken in his department and their relation to other company divisions. (Developing Managerial Skills in engineers and Scientist, 1995, p. 6)

11. Technical Specialist/Engineer: For the purpose of this study, the following definition was used to apply to individuals who posses the educational qualifications and work experience, along with any legal certifications that were required by engineering schools, and employers.

12. Transitionee: for the purpose of this study simply means that an individual thinking about transitioning, in the process of transition, or has newly transition into the management competency.

13. Transition: Is defined as a passing from one condition, form, stage activity from one state to another. (Webster's Third New World Dictionary, 1991, p. 1420). For the purpose of this study this term ill refer to the TS transitioning to PM. By this transition the TS was in a new job title and with it new duties accompanied such.

14. You: for the purpose of this study is that individual making that transition into management or contemplating the move.

<u>Overview of Study</u>

The overview of this study was based on the tradition of exploratory studies with qualitative interviews, this study is to achieve a better understanding of the challenge and difficulties that the technical specials in the federal government experience while in their chosen profession as a TS and once the decision was made that they were ready to progress or was recommended for the management competency the newly acquired skills needed to become a successful manager. Through the interviewing process it is the intensions of this writer to have participants provide narratives on the topic questions posed. This narrative will provide insight on the individuals experience and what was felt with each. Once this data is gathered this writer will identify the commonalities. Those commonalities topics will be formulated to provide the most relative issues each interviewee had. Exploration is particularly useful when researchers lack a clear idea of the problems they will meet during the study (Cooper, 2003, p.151). This study examined key issues that were thought to be the most common in the transition of the technical specialist into program management within the D.O.D.

Chapter 2

Review of Related Literature

Introduction

This chapter is a review of related literature that is relevant to this research. It will look at a case study from Hill (2003), which describes transitions from other chosen professional careers. The chapter will also discuss the skills required for management by leading experts in the field though literature readings. Furthermore, the chapter will include a brief history and overview of the three most well known management practices that still are in use today they are Classical, Behavioral and the Management Science School this writer will introduce the contributors that are mainly responsible for these methods. The first topic will begin with the evolution of management. The second topic will begin with essential skills needed for transitions into management and what managers should focus on. The third topic will be related to this study about transitions into management as Hill's (2003) studies formed the basis for the study.

Brief History of Management Overview

Topic One: Evolution of Management: the three most well known

Classical—one of the first schools of management thought was the classical management theory. This theory was developed during the Industrial Revolution when problems related to factory systems began to appear. The problem developed from managers not knowing how to train their employees many of which did not speak English due to them being immigrates. Also managers did not know how to deal with the increase of labor dissatisfactions. So an effort began to test solutions and as of that result so did the classical management theory. As the theory developed to find the "one best way" (Modern Management, 1998) to manage and perform task from this school of thought two segments developed one being the classical scientific and the classical administrative.

For the purpose of this study we will discuss the primary three contributors, among many other valuable contributors. This writer will look at Fredrick Taylor for the scientific method and Henri Fayol and Mary Parker Follett for the classical administrative thought.

The **classical scientific method** arose due the need to increase productivity and efficiency. The main focus was on trying to find the best way of getting the most work done by examining how the process of work was being accomplished and by closely scrutinizing the skills of the workforce.

The "father of scientific management" as he was so often called Frederick Taylor (1856–1915) believed that organizations should study task and then thereby develop a precise procedure. His main goal was to increase workers productivity and efficiency by scientifically designing jobs. His basic thought was that there was one best way to doing the job and once discovered that job should be put into operation. (Certo, 1997, p.30). One of Taylor's best-known examples of this way was with the Bethlehem Steel Co. When Taylor introduced his scientific method and his management philosophy on how he modified the job of the employees whose sole purpose was the shoveling of materials at the company.

During the modification process, Taylor made assumptions that any workers job could be reduced to a science. So he constructed the "science of shoveling," to obtain answers he observed and experimented with the following questions:

1. Will a first-class worker do more with more per day with a shovel of 5, 10, 15, 20, 30, or 40 pounds?

2. What kinds of shovels work best with which materials?

3. How quickly can a shovel be pushed into a pile of materials and pulled out when properly loaded?

4. How much time is required to swing a shovel backward and throw the load a given horizontal distance at a given height?

As these answers were formulated, Taylor was able to develop insights on how to increase the total amount of materials shoveled per day and by matching the shovel size with the size of the worker and the other parameters of the study the efficiency of the worker raise his shovel and once implemented the companies numbers had been reduced from 600 to 140.

To give a little more insight of the study this writer will list some of basic ideas from some of the other contributors in regards to scientific management development. They include the following:

- Developing new standards in methods for doing each job

- Selecting, training, and developing workers instead of allowing them to chose their own task themselves

- Developing a spirit of cooperation between workers and management to ensure that work is carried out in accordance with devised procedures

- Dividing work between workers and management in almost equal shares, with each group taking over the work for which it is best fitted (Modern Management, 1997).

The **classical administrative approach** focus was on the total organizations with emphasis on the development of managerial principles rather than on work methods. For the purpose of this study two contributors will be discussed by this writer they are Henri Fayol and Mary Parker Follett. This theorist studied the flow of information within an organization by placing importance on the understanding how organizations operated.

Due to his writings on the elements and general management principles and is usually regarded as the "Pioneer of administrative theory" (Certo, 1997, p. 35). Henri Fayol (1841–1925) outlined the elements of management and is still worthwhile divisions under which to study. Fayol was a French mining engineer who developed what is known as the 14 principles of management based on his management experiences. These principles are still used today in modern day with managers with general guidelines on how a supervisor should organize their department and mange their staff. Although, later research has created some controversy over the following principals they are still widely used in management theories.

The 14 principals are listed in the following:

1. Division of work: Division of work and specialization produces more and better work with same effort.

2. Authority and responsibility: Authority is the right to give orders and the power to exact obedience. A manager has official authority because of his or her position, as well as personal authority based on individual personality, intelligence, and experience. Authority creates responsibility.

3. Discipline: Obedience and respect within an organization are absolutely essential. Good discipline requires managers to apply sanctions whenever violations become apparent.

4. Unity of command: Workers should receive orders from only one manager.

5. Unity of direction: The entire organization should be moving towards a common objective, in a common direction.

6. Subordination of individual interests to general interests: The interest of one person should not take priority over the interest of the organization as a whole.

7. Remuneration of personnel: Salaries—the price of services rendered by employees—should be fair and provide satisfaction both to the employee and employer.

8. Centralization: the objective is the best utilization of personnel. The degree of centralization varies according to the dynamics of each organization.

9. Scalar Chain: A chain of authority exists from the highest organizational authority to the lowest.

10. Order: Organizational order for materials and personnel is essential. The right materials and the right employees are necessary for each organizational function and activity.

11. Equity: All employees should be treated as equally if possible.

12. Stability of tenure of personnel: To attain the maximum productivity of personnel, a stable work force is needed.

13. Initiative: Management should take steps to encourage worker initiative, which is defined as a new or additional activity undertaken through self-direction.

14. Esprit de corps: Teamwork is fundamentally important to an organization. Work teams and extensive face-to-face verbal communication encourages teamwork. (Modern Management, 1997).

To round off the thought of the classical administrative approach this writer will include Mary Parker Follett (1868–1933) as she stressed the importance of an organization establishing common goals for its employees. However, she began to think a little differently than other theorist discarding the notion of a command style of management were "employees are treated like robots" (Certo, 1997, p. 16) to talking about issues as ethics, power, and leadership. Follet encouraged managers to allow employees to participate in the decision making process.

Furthermore, she stressed the importance of people rather than techniques—a concept well before her time. As a result, management "scholars" of her same era didn't take a pioneer like her to seriously. Because of this the writer felt it necessary to include her in this research because so much of what managers do today is based on the fundamentals she established more than 70 years ago.

Classical Approach Limitations

Even the contributors felt compelled and were encouraged to write about their managerial experiences mainly due to the success they enjoyed. Structuring work to be more efficient and defining the manager's role more precisely yielded many substantial improvements in productivity, by which Taylor and Fayol were quick to document. However, this approach does not adequately emphasize the human variables.

In today's organizations people do not seem to be as influenced by bonuses as they were in the nineteenth century. It has been said and generally agreed to that critical interpersonal area, such as conflict, communication, leadership, and motivation, were shortchanged in the classical approach. (Certo, 1997, p.37). Due to this management research continued into the 20th century and questions arose regarding the interactions and motivations of the individual within the organization.

The management principles developed during this time simply were not useful and could not explain employee motivation and behavior at work. As a result, the behavioral school was a natural outgrowth of this revolutionary management experiment.

Classical Schools Approach Evaluation

Developers of the classical managerial theory met the needs of an expanding industrial world. By them examining the *management of work*, individual worker productivity was improved and organizations could and did very much benefit, acquiring greater resources from the increased profitability and growth.

Those who examined the *management of the organization* created a growing awareness of the nature of managerial functioning within the organization and thereby enhanced the ability to manage the contemporary and increasingly complex organization. Managers were now attempting to determine the necessary skills for the managerial task and were experimenting with methods of teaching these skills. (Montana & Charnov, 2000, p.22)

Largely those with an engineering background, who had asserted that the key to workers efficiency and organizational productivity was efficient job design, the use of appropriate incentives, and effective managerial functioning, formulated this Classical Approach to management theory. This was perceived as a formal and impersonal approach to management and was resisted by many workers because it failed to take into account the human dimensions of an organization. But nevertheless the contributions of the Classical Theory of management are still used by today's successful managers.

Behavioral management theory is often referred to the human relations movement because its focus was on the human dimension of work. Behavior theorist strongly believed that a better understanding of human behavior at work, such as motivation, conflict, expectations, and group dynamics, improved productivity.

The contributors to this school of thought viewed employees as individuals, resources, and as assets to be developed and worked with—not as machines, as in the past. There has been several individuals and experiments contributed to this theory.

For the purpose of this study this writer will discuss one contributor Abraham Maslow (1908–1970). He was a practicing psychologist, and developed one of the most widely used need theories; the theory of motion was based on the consideration of human needs. He had three assumptions to his theory they were as follows:

- Human needs are never completely satisfied.

- Human behavior is purposeful and is motivated by the needs for satisfaction.

- Needs can be classified according to a hierarchical structure of importance, from the lowest to the highest. (Donnnelly, Gibson, Ivancevich, 1981, p.220)

Maslow also wrote and broke down the hierarchical needs into five areas they are as follows:

- Physiological needs. Maslow grouped all physical needs necessary for maintaining basic human well being, such as food and drink, into this category. However, after the need is satisfied it no longer is a motivator. Maslow once stated" a person who is lacking food, safety, love, and esteem would probably hunger for food more strongly than anything else" (Donnnelly, Gibson, Ivancevich, 1981, p.220)

- Safety needs: this included the need for basic security, stability, protection, and freedom from fear. A normal state exists for an individual to have all these needs generally satisfied. Otherwise, they become primary motivators.

- Social needs: these needs are for companionship after the physical and safety need are satisfied and are no longer motivators, the need for belonging and love emerges as a primary motivator. Individuals strive for or try to establish meaningful relationships with significant others.

- Esteem needs: Individuals must develop self-confidence and wants to achieve status, reputation, fame, and glory.

- Self-actualization: Assuming all of the previous needs are met or satisfied, an individual needs to find himself.

Maslow was instrumental in his hierarchy of needs theory that has helped managers visualize employee's motivation. There have been other contributors to the behavior management theory this writer will give a brief mention to those for anyone wanting to continue further research. One being Elton Mayo (1880–1949) from the well know Hawthorne studies. And Douglas McGregor (1906–1964) who was extremely influenced by both the Hawthorne studies and Maslow. McGregor is known for the Theory X and Y.

As a group of theorists they discovered that people worked for inner satisfaction and not materialistic rewards. Thus, shifting the focus to the role of the individuals in an organization's performance.

Behavioral School Approach Evaluation

This approach was to better understand the workers behavior therefore; productivity improvement has had a powerful impact on U.S. management thought. It provided many insights into organizational behavior and still continues to have a major impact on the direction for those engaged in organization theory research. This approach has given rise to effective management skills training and development efforts in virtually every major American business. From this it has created a more sophisticated and a more effective style on the manager's role when dealing with the human variables in the work place. (Montana & Charnov, 2000, p.27)

Management Science Approach

This approach was derived by the quantitative approach bought on by studies that were conducted during World War II. During this time mathematicians, physicist, and other scientists joined together to solve military problems and the quantitative school a management was the result. This method used quantitative techniques, such as statistics, information models, and computer simulations to improve decision-making. Today, this view encourages managers to use mathematics, statistics, and other quantitative techniques to make decisions. The following is a list of what mangers may use for science applications:

- Mathematical forecasting helps make projections that are useful in the planning process.

- Inventory modeling helps control inventories by mathematically establishing how and when to order a product.

- Queuing theory helps allocate service or workstations to minimize customer waiting and service cost.

However, the group of contributors approached these managerial problems into two assumptions:

1. Applying the scientific method can solve all problems that characterize a system.

2. Solving mathematical equations that represent the system can solve these systems problems.

This approach may also be heard as Operations management (OR) even though a narrow branch of the quantitative methods to management it focused on managing the process of transforming materials, labor, and capital into useful goods or services. OR today is primarily interested in quality.

For the purpose of this study the writer will conclude this section with **systems management theory,** which had a significant effect on management service. This was a system that had s interrelated set of elements which made it's functioning whole. It is important to realize an organization as a system that is composed of four elements:

- Inputs—material or human resources
- Transformation processes—technological and managerial processes
- Outputs—products or services
- Feedback—reactions from the environment

In the relationship to the organization, *inputs* include resources such as raw materials, money, technologies, and most of all people. These inputs are then integrated into a transformation process where they are planned, organized, motivated, and controlled to ultimately meet the organizational goals.

The one thing that one should remember about Management Science, also known as Operations Research, is that it is an approach to management that maintains that productivity can be improved and organizational effectiveness increased by means of the scientific method and the use of mathematical models. (Montana & Charnov, 2000, p.28)

Management Science Approach Evaluation

Management science techniques are widely used in contemporary industries to improve worker productivity. This scientific approach stresses a *systems approach* that views the total operating system and analyzes a problem within that system.

The problem is seen to exist as it relates to the total system, and any proposed solution is evaluated as it relates to the same system. Any course of action that solves a production problem but that also causes more problems for the organization will more than likely be rejected.

Despite the success at solving complex production problems, Operations Research has been criticized for its focus on production and the lack of focus relative to the worker and the human dimensions of the management function. Furthermore, many problems in modern business today however complex require an even wider perspective than that offered by a system wide OR approach, which often fails to account for unanticipated opportunity or environmental threats.

Operations management skills of analysis and solutions determinations are often viewed as operational skills, and not management skills. There is more often than not a gap between the *technical expertise* in management science and that of scientists in managerial skills.

However, OR has made and will continue to make a valuable contributions to management practice and its techniques have been proven extremely useful.

Brief History of DAWIA

In 1990, Congress passed the Defense Acquisition Workforce Improvement Act. The Act's intent is to ensure that DOD has qualified personnel to manage the acquisitions of defense systems. Skilled personnel are needed to meet the challenges associated with defense systems that have become increasingly complex and costly.

The birth of formal acquisition began in the 1940"s and the need for highly qualified personnel have been recognized. As time passed, there was an increasing demand for these personnel to have more sophisticated competencies. Today's professional must posses increasing levels of:

1. Specialized knowledge

2. Analytical skills

3. Good judgment.

The vast majority of Technical Specialist is of an engineering background and being such this study uses related materials that might enlighten transitions of technologist into a management career. The reference material for this study was very limited. This writer was at a loss to find in the department of defense within the federal government when it came to transitioning from a technical discipline to a management discipline.

Topic Two: Essential skills needed for the transition to management

Through this writer's research a common theme appears when it comes to what skills are required to becoming a manager. If the professional were aware of these skills early on he or she would be much better prepared for their transition in to the field of management.

The first part of this topic will discuss functions of management, followed by seven traits or characteristics of what a good manager ought to know. If the Transitionee has knowledge of as these principles he or she should experience a successful transitioning. It is this writer's beliefs that upon completion of this study the Transitionee once made aware of these fundamentals of management and they would have a better knowledge of what the expectations of themselves would be and would provide them a solid ground of which to start from due to their newly enhanced knowledge and understanding of these traits or characteristics that would greatly benefit the Transitionee for what may lay ahead. Therefore, this will be less stressful allowing them to enjoy their new responsibilities and to better antiquate them due to the skills in which they studied. And from these newly acquired skills they have a better understanding of what maybe expected from them in their new roles in the management competency.

Functions of Management

Again let's look back to Fayol and what his theories brought out. He developed four functions that were performed by management and they are as follows:

- Planning
- Organizing
- Controlling
- Leading

Each of these functions will be discussed in the sections that follow.

Planning, Planning is the process of developing a philosophy of managing (i.e., management beliefs, values, and attitudes), setting objectives, establishing goals, and devising short-and long-range strategies to achieve them.

Organizing, The organizing function is the process of achieving coordinated effort through the creation of a structure of task and authority relationships.

Controlling, Controlling is the process of establishing standards of performance, evaluating actual performance against these standards, and correcting deviations from standards and plans.

Leading, Leadership entails influencing a group's activities to accomplish certain goals. It involves behavior of both the leader and followers.

The above statements of the four function definitions were from Badawy (1995, p9). Michael K. Badawy wrote literature on the development of managerial skills in engineers and scientist, and succeeding as a technical manager. His works will be stated throughout this writer's paper as well as B. Michael Aucoin who wrote from engineer to manager, mastering the transition (2002)

The Seven Success Principles for Transitioning into management

Throughout, this writer's researches seven main success principles continue to appear from all of the many books and text reviewed. Every aspect of transitioning into a management had on average six of the seven principals that will be discussed next.

As well known as Fayol's 14 functions on principles of management are and is spoken about in topic one of this chapter. And stated, this researcher found seven common principles in the numerous books and texts read and for this purpose would be discussed.

The focus seemed to be on seven fundamental principles that if followed will substantially improve the success and satisfaction of the transition to management.

They are as follows:

- Communication
- Conflicts

- Delegating

- Motivation

- Performance

- Relationships

- Stress

The good news is that the mastery of these principles and the successful exercise of them is a goal that can be readily achieved by a technologist. "Technical management skills don't just happen by chance; nor are they the attributes of specially gifted people. Rather, they can be developed systematically" (Thamhain, 1992, p 42)

Aucoin (2002) stated the transition from engineer to manager is a challenging journey. The success skills required of a manager are far different from those required of an engineer. Many engineers are blindsided by the difficulties of the transition and experience considerable distress because of it. (p. 8)

- **Communication:** a method used to convey both thoughts and feelings. Communication is utilized to influence others, inform others and to express feelings. (Buhler, 2001, p286)

On the surface communication may seem like an extremely simple process. However, in actuality this is an extraordinarily complex one. It is fraught with pitfalls and barriers. Seldom are people effective in their communication. Instead, people and managers generally make false assumptions or they pay little attention to the complexities of the communication process.

This writer will discuss some of the issues related to the communication problem so that a better understanding of it can help the transitions into the managerial field.

- Barriers to Communication—Physical separation creates barriers to effective communication. Even with the technologies of today with the use of computers and phones, the richness of face—face communication is lost. This reduces the effectiveness due to the many nonverbal and emotional elements in the process, which are never seen or felt.

- Nonverbal Communication—This communication process is comprised of more than just the spoken word. The old saying "Actions speak louder than words" is so true. The gestures you use, your body language, your gender, your dress, and the very tone of your voice all add up to the part of delivering the communication. Some times these are the only components to the communication process. Nonverbal communication includes all communication that is conveyed without words. The key is to use nonverbal component to complement the verbal component. Some other factors to consider for the management Transitionee are as follows for even further considerations to the nonverbal realm.

  - *Proxemics* is the study of how space is used. This includes what is known as comfort zones that surround an individuals' personal space and even the dynamics of seating in a business setting. (Buhler, 2001, p.289).

  - *Kinesics* is the study of body language. Body language can communicate everything from anxiety to primping. Your posture also communicates a great about you. Facial cues are critical to the communication process. Your face often times gives a real sense of the message right away. (Buhler, 2001, p.290).

- Active Listening—Contrary to what any may think listening is an active skill. This however is not a passive process—if it is to be effective. "Good listeners are at a premium". (Buhler, 2001, p.291).

Listening is a critical skill in the communication process. It greatly impacts your ability to be more effective a manager. Empathic listeners understand the message and the feelings being communicated.

- **Conflict**—Commonly occurs when people are not involved in change efforts in the organization. As this writer discusses this key principal as in the seven as a manager in transitions he or she must be aware of conflicts within the organization they are inevitable when people come together. The potential for conflict is found everyday virtually everywhere. In a managerial term it is simply stated. "Conflict occurs when one person wants one outcome that will prevent others from getting the outcome that they want" (Buhler, 2001, p.129). As people are denied their desired outcomes, conflicts will result. This conflict can occur in varying degrees-being either minor or major.

Conflict holds generally a negative connotation. Yet there are real benefits to be gained from optimal levels of conflict in the organization. There are many types of conflicts such as functional vs. dysfunctional they can include (1) Interpersonal, (2) Intergroup, (3) Interorganziational, and (4) Intrapersonal. For the purpose of this study this writer will discuss the aspect of management being successful in conflicts as the transitionalist from a given profession into the management realm within ones owns organization the knowledge of principles in this section will better inform them on the techniques used to achieve conflicts successfully through management resolutions.

As managers, you will spend an inordinate amount of time resolving conflict. Certain skills and abilities can make you more successful in dealing with conflict. "Fact is managers spend on average 21 percent of their time or one day a week, dealing with conflict" (Buhler, 2001, p.134). Let's begin by saying first and foremost to be successful in conflict management you must consider your attitude. You must strive to maintain and keep a positive attitude. You must understand and recognize that some conflict could be and is beneficial for you, your employees, and your organization.

Disagreement is healthy. In addition, you must keep emotions in check. You cannot let your emotions rule the process. It has been heavily recognized that anger is part of conflict resolution it cannot be the primary emotion ruling the process. Furthermore, you must be assertive to be successful in conflict management. That means you must be able to stand up for yourself and your rights. Yet, as hard as it maybe at the same time, you cannot violate the rights of others. This is a fine line always keep in mind that the nonassertive individual (also referred to as being passive) lets other people's rights become more important than their own. In turn this person generally has little respect and is not as effective in conflict management.

However, moving over to the far extreme is just as ineffective. The aggressive person violates the rights of others. They tend to think that their own rights take precedence over others. Their main focus is on wanting and getting control at all cost.

As you can begin to see this is why this writer found it to be one of the major principles in resolving conflict management processes, there are many required skills and abilities needed to manage conflicts. Consider the following skills to help you to effectively manage conflicts, which this writer felt important enough to list. The nine of them they are as follows:

- Strive for a win-win solution. It takes more energy and creative thinking, but is more likely to address the root cause of the problem.

- Value everyone's viewpoint. Don't jump to conclusions, but hear everyone out and try to see each party's perspective of the conflict. It requires empathy to recognize everyone's ideas.

- Be respectful of everyone involved. You should not let personalities influence you. Treat all parties with equal levels of respect.

- Consider personnel changes as a last resort. People can be transferred out of conflict.

- Make a conscious choice on your part to cooperate. It is too easy to set up competitive situations. You are responsible for creating a cooperative environment with the parties.

- Exercise patience. Speedy solutions are usually not win-win outcomes. You must also exercise patience with all parties involved as they present their viewpoints.

- Part of being patient may require that you step back from the situation. Instead wanting to rush to judgment, it may very well be appropriate in some situations to gain a different perspective by stepping back. The process can then be restarted with a fresh view.

- Depersonalize the conflict. You must help the parties involved to remain focused on the facts and be objective. You can play an instrumental role in helping the parties identify the points of agreement rather than focusing on point of the disagreement.

- Recognize that solving conflicts can be a very painful process for everyone involved. Feedback is an important part of the process of conflict resolution, but you and the other parties involved may not necessarily like the feedback once received.

However, remember when managing conflict, it is important to recognize that different conflict is created as a result of different power relationships within the organization. Understanding the power relationship may be the first step towards understanding the conflict. Buhler (2001) indicated,"Managing conflict is not the same as avoiding conflict. Rather, it is dealing with the conflict in a constructive way". (p.135)

This writer finds this section very important and will talk on other conflict issues such as a conflict with your upper management or with your equal in the level of management. This writer will convey how to discuss those issues of conflict within the six principles. Then, this writer would like to conclude the conflict portion with controlling conflict and then as the final issue of stimulating conflict. Everything this writer is studying and believes though this research; the technical specialist or any other profession can learn that the transition into management can be easier with the proper skills sets and mindset of these skills.

As the name indicates, the balance of power is even in even-power relationships. The parties involved in the conflict are at the same organizational level with equal power. This type of conflict is usually set up in a win-lose situation and it is upon you to restructure it into a win-win situation.

However, the high-low power relationship is much more difficult. This is where one party has a more powerful position then the other party. The balance is in favor of the more powerful individual, who is trying to control the other, less powerful one. Hierarchical differences often create resentment toward the authority figure. In the high-middle-low status relationship characterizes your managerial position. In this case the middle party is being squeezed from both sides with increasing hostility from all sides. However, there are specific steps that you should consider when discussing the conflict issue. These are as follows:

1. Begin by defining the problem. Just as in the relational problem-solving model, it becomes critical to identify the cause (instead of the symptoms).

2. Gather information. This step identifies what is really involved in the situation. There is a fact-finding mission to shed light on the issue.

3. Present solutions. Brainstorming is an important step, which generates creative alternatives. This gets a lot of open ideas on the table.

4. Identify the goal. This is a critical step in determining what the solution should achieve. The bottom line: You must know what both parties want.

5. Choose a solution. Do not start at this step. Starting at this step is a mistake that will short-change the process and may create the probability that the out come may not be as successful. Selecting the solution requires that you keep in mind the goal. You then select the solution that is most feasible by narrowing down the alternatives that fit the goal.

6. Finally, you must implement the solution. The implementation also involves determining timetables, establishing measures for following up, or monitoring the implementation to ensure that the goal identified is achieved.

- Controlling Conflict—As a manager, you have the responsibility to help manage conflicts before it gets to the stage of resolution. You can manage the environment that sets the stage for conflict and minimize the probability of conflict that must be resolved. This can be done in a number of ways. It requires the monitoring of the organizational climate and watching for situations that are ripe for dysfunctional conflict.

By using creative methods, many times you can enlarge the resource pool. Because if the resources are scarce and their allocations often open the door for conflict, you may manage the situation be making a larger resource pool or providing additional resources. Sometimes it can mean just transferring funds or reallocating the resources for which you have responsibility.

Buhler (2001) once stated, "An integrator can be used as a liaison position. This neutral third party can help open up the communication between two departments in conflict" (p.137).

Usually, conflict is created as a result of interdependent task. You can improve the coordination of these interdependent tasks to minimize the possibility of conflict.

The following are other suggestions in trying to control conflicts:

- Developing superordinate goals alleviates the conflict created by competing goals. An example, instead of fighting over whose goals are achieved, both goals are set aside for a higher-order organizational goal. Both parties then learn that they must work together to get resolution—otherwise, a lose-lose situation could result.

- Focusing on a common goal creates the realization that both sides more alike than originally thought.

- Pay attention to how well the employee personalities fit into the organization. Personality testing can be used in the selection process. Care can also be taken when selecting team members and establishing work groups to ensure that fewer conflicts occur.

Let this writer conclude this section with a brief thought on sometimes stimulating conflict, as is what an organization may need. As there are organizations that need some optimal level of conflict, it is possible that you may need to stimulate conflict in some situations. While conflict management is generally thought of in terms of diminishing the level of conflict, the flip side is as equally important. Because some conflict is healthy for the organization, you must be able to stimulate conflict when sufficient levels are not present.

When stimulating conflict, you may need to set up competitive situations in order to create conflict. Many organizations use sales contest among units to stimulate this competition. Retailers frequently develop sales contest among stores to stimulate rivalry.

However, proceed with caution. And extreme care must be taken when stimulating conflict. This conflict can cross the line and actually become destructive to the organization. Such as when sales contest are used, they can easily get out of hand and generate dysfunctional levels of conflict.

- Outsiders can be imported into the organization. Because of new blood which often stimulates conflict and encourages new ideas and creativity.

- Revising the way things are being done stimulates conflict. Changing procedures opens the door to challenging the status quo. Keeping things the same creates complacency, and can become dysfunctional as levels of conflict diminish to destructive levels.

Again, this writer found the research encountered in these seven principles to stand out from all others in the successful transitioning into a management competency. This researcher feels after reading and absorbing these seven principles your transition will be much more enjoyable and more stress free. Your abilities and newfound knowledge has prepared you for the challenges of your new career path in the management arena.

- **Delegating**—This concept is closely linked with authority. Delegation is the downward transfer of authority from a manager to a subordinate. In today's time most organizations encourage managers to delegate authority in order to provide maximum flexibility in meeting customer needs.

  In addition, delegation leads to empowerment, in that people have the freedom to contribute ideas and do their jobs in other possible ways. This involvement can increase job satisfaction for the individual and frequently results in much better job performance.

  Without delegation, managers do all the work themselves and underutilize their workers. The ability to delegate is crucial to managerial success. This writer found this to be one of the hardest principles for the new manager to grasp, as they wanted to continue hands on approach that just isn't the case once you have crossed the line into the management competency.

This writer will discuss the four steps managers should take if they want to be truly successful in delegating responsibilities to their teams. They are as follows:

1. Specifically assign tasks to individuals team members. The manager needs to make sure that employees know that they are ultimately responsible for carrying out specific assignments.

2. Give team members the correct amount of authority to accomplish assignments. Typically, an employee is assigned authority commensurate with the task. A classical principle of organization warns managers not to delegate without giving the subordinate the authority to perform and to delegate the task. When an employee has responsibility for the task outcome but has little authority, accomplishing the job is possible but normally very difficult. The subordinate without authority must rely on persuasion and luck to meet the performance expectations. However, when an employee has authority exceeding responsibility, he or she may become a tyrant, using authority toward frivolous outcomes.

3. Make sure that the team members accept responsibility. Responsibility is the flip side of authority coin. Responsibility is the duty to perform the task or activity an employee has been assigned. An important distinction between authority and responsibility is that the supervisor or manager delegate's authority, but the responsibility is shared. Delegation of authority gives a subordinate the right to make commitments, use resources, and take actions in relation to the duties assigned. Furthermore, in making this delegation, the obligation created is not shifted from the supervisor or manager to the subordinate—it is shared. A supervisor or manager always

retains some responsibilities for the work performed by lower-level units or individuals.

4.   Create accountability. Team members need to know that they are held accountable for their projects. Accountability means answering for one's actions and accepting the consequences. Team members may need to report and justify task outcomes to their supervisors or manager. Managers can build accountability into their organizations by monitoring performances and rewarding successful outcomes. Although managers are encouraged to delegate authority, they often find accomplishing this step difficult for the following reasons:

- Delegation requires planning, and planning takes time. A manager may say, "By the time I explain this task to someone, I could do it myself." This manager is overlooking the fact that even though the initial time spent up front training someone to do a task may save much more time in the long run. Once an employee has learned how to do a task, the manager will not have to take the time to show that employee how to do it again. This improves the flow of the process from that point forward. (Certo, 1997, p. 262)

- Managers may simply lack the confidence in the abilities of their subordinates. Such a situation fosters the attitude, "If you want it done well, do it yourself." If managers feel that their subordinates lack ability, they need to provide appropriate training so that all are comfortable performing their duties.

- Managers experience dual accountability. Managers are accountable for their own actions and the actions of their subordinates. If a subordinate fails to perform a certain task or does so poorly, the manager is ultimately responsible for the subordinate's failure. But by the same token, if the subordinate is successful, the manager shares in that success as well, the department can be even more productive.

- Finally, managers may refrain from delegating because they are insecure about their value to the organization. However, managers need to realize that they become more valuable as their teams become more productive and talented.

This writer wants to spend time in this section, as despite the perceived disadvantages of delegation, the true reality is that a manger can improve the performance of his or her work groups by empowering subordinates through effective delegation. Few managers are successful in the long term without learning to delegate more effectively.

This writer will attempt through the research to discuss what managers must learn to delegate effectively. The following principles may be helpful for managers and those in transition to management. Again, it is the intension of this writer to give the best choices and the knowledge needed for a successful transition into the world of management. The additional four principles are as follows:

- Principle 1: Match the employee to the task. Managers should carefully consider the employees to whom they delegate tasks. The individual selected should possess the skills and capabilities needed to complete the task. Perhaps even more important, is to delegate to an individual who is not only able to complete the task but also willing to complete the task. Therefore, managers should delegate to employees who will view their accomplishments as personal benefits.

- Principle 2: Be organized and communicate clearly. The manager must have a clear understanding of what needs to be done, what deadlines exist, and what the special; skill set are required. Furthermore, managers must be capable of communicating their instructions effectively if their subordinates are to perform up to their expectations.

- Principle 3: Transfer authority and accountability with the task. This is a very important principle to remember. The delegation process is doomed to failure if the individual to whom the task is delegated is not given the authority to succeed at accomplishing the task and is not held accountable for the results as well.

Managers must expect employees to carry the ball and then let them do so. This simply means providing the employees with the necessary resources and power to succeed, giving them timely feedback on their progress, and holding them fully accountable for the results of their efforts. Managers also should be available to answer questions as needed.

- Principle 4: Choose the level of delegation carefully. Delegation does not mean that a manager can walk away from the task or the person to whom the task is delegated. The manager must maintain some control of both the process and the results of the delegated activities. Depending upon the confidence the manager has in the subordinate and the importance of the task, the manager can choose to delegate at several levels.

For the purpose of this study this writer will conclude the delegation portion here. Since these are the views this writer was the most important feature of the research. It is of this researchers belief strongly feels with this information the transitions into management can be better understood.

- **Motivation**—Is at the heart and is a critical issue for managers and will determine your success. Because management is all about getting things done through others, the ability to get others to perform is essential and critical. The workplace motivation that you are most concerned with is the high level of performance that results in meeting (or exceeding) organizational objectives. With downsizing and restructuring being commonplace today in organizations, employee moral has been negatively impacted. Some have even gone so far as to suggest that employee morale is at a very critically low point. This has made the motivation of the workforce even more important.

The old techniques of yester year of motivating no longer apply or work in today's environment. The old method of command and control are not effective with the team concept. Providing a one-size-fits-all rewards no longer work with the diverse workforce of today.

Therefore, you must use sound concepts to more effectively to motivate your employees. This begins with an understanding of how motivation theories can be applied to better encourage and to spark motivation in your workforce.

These theories can provide you with the motivational levers to pull from in order to increase the motivation of your employees.

Motivation is not a personal characteristic that people possess. Rather, motivation varies as the situation changes. You motivation and your employees' motivation will vary from situation to situation. Buhler (2001) indicates, "Research has indicated that the average employee works at only 60 percent of their capacity. Effective motivation techniques can improve this statistic by tapping into the 40 percent of unused potential". (p. 158).

Motivation refers to the processes that determine how much effort will be expended to perform the job. Motivation is a very complex issue, and people's behaviors are driven by more than one motive at a time. This writer suggests you refresh yourself with topic one of this paper to learn some of those motivation theories.

The success of your organization depends upon the success of each individual within the organization. Believe it when this writer says that motivation is a critical driving force in ones organizational performance. A lack of motivation will cost the company in its revenue in terms of lost productivity and missed opportunities. People are more inclined to deliver performance that is manually acceptable. Some have even wondered today if Americans are still in search of excellence or if they are in search of mediocrity instead.

Motivation is an extremely complex issue requiring an understanding of individuals. It is no longer answered with just money. In the past, a manager might be able to throw additional money at an employee to improve motivation. However, money today doesn't get the same mileage in today's workplace.

In not so distant past, the motivation tactic was to scare. "Do it or else…" was the refrain of the command-and-control manager. That tactic no longer works in today's environment of empowerment and teams.

Remember to study topic one of this writer's paper on motivation theories, there is a good amount to look at from Maslow, to Herzberg, to McGregor, to McClelland to Adams, to Vroom all of which have been contributors to management.

- **Performance** is included, the seven principles are due to, and once you have gotten a handle on motivation you must continue to monitor their performance. Thus, the need for an appraisal system is needed.

For the purpose of this study this writer will not go into great detail but will be brief enough so that you will have a better understanding of managing performance. To make the new transitionee into management aware of some of the other duties in which he or she will have to include in their daily management function.

- You must admit to the fact that your employees are one of the greatest assets or resource to your organization. They continue, however, to be one of the most mismanaged resources in most of the organizations of today. If you effectively gain the benefits from an effective performance management organization the rewards will be tremendous.

- Performance Appraisal—The process of reviewing individuals' past productivity to evaluate the contribution they have made toward attaining management system objectives. Training, performance appraisal—which is also called *performance reviews* and *performance evaluation*—is a continuing activity that focuses on both established human resources within the organization and newcomers. Its main purpose is to furnish feedback to organization members about how they can become more productive and useful to the organization in its quest for excellence. (Certo, 1997, p 290).

There are several methods of performance appraisals table 1 describes several methods of the system.

Table 1
Descriptions of Several Methods of Performance Appraisals

APPRAISAL METHOD	DESCRIPTION
Rating Scale	Individuals appraising performance use a form containing several employees' qualities and characteristics to be evaluated (e.g., dependability, initiative, leadership). Each evaluated on a scale from 1–7
Employee comparisons	Appraisers rank employees according to such factors as job performance and value to the organization. Only one employee can occupy a particular ranking.
Free-form essay	Appraisers simply write down their impressions of employees in a paragraph form
Critical-form essay	Appraisers write down particularly good or bad events involving employees as these occur. Records of all documented events for any one employee are used to evaluate that person's performance

This writer will now discuss why to use performance appraisals. As stated throughout this study this writers' intension is to give the transitionee into the management realm the most important principles this researcher found. Most U.S. firms today are engaged in some form of a performance appraisal system. Douglas McGregor suggested the following three reasons for using performance appraisals: (Carroll, 1987, pp. 7-15)

1. They provide systematic judgments to support salary increases, promotions, transfers, and sometimes demotions or terminations.

2. They are a means of telling subordinates how they are doing and of suggesting needed changes in behavior, attitudes, skills, or job knowledge; they let subordinates know where they stand with the boss.

3. They furnish a useful basis for the coaching and counseling of individuals by superiors.

In concluding this principle let the writer leaves you with this. The performance appraisal process is an opportunity to increase the worth of the employee through constructive feedback, as a means of rewarding or punishing the employee through positive or negative comments. Paper work should be viewed only as an aid in providing this feedback, not as an end in itself. Also great care should be taken to make appraisal feedback as tactful and objective as possible to minimize negative reactions.

- **Relationships**—Are now more important than ever since businesses are now becoming more relationship-oriented. And these relationships are very much part of the management process they are so critical that this writer had included it into the seven principles.

At the heart of these skills is an understanding of individuals within and outside the organization. Human-relations are more then just common sense. It requires that you understand your behavior and the behavior of those with whom you interact.

Managers occupy boundary-spanning positions responsible for the developing of relationships both internally and externally. These external relationships are established across organizational borders.

This is a very deep subject matter and could be expanded upon this principle in a complete chapter in itself. However, this writer will attempt to give the transitionee an overview of what is perceived to be the most successful keys or thoughts for relationship management. Let's begin with the following:

- Perception—Is probably the single most key in the understanding relationships in the work place. Everyone doesn't respond in the same way or manner to the world around him or her; perception is very much subjective. Everyone picks and chooses different stimuli to pay attention to, and they interpret these stimuli differently. Perception is simply your interpretation of reality.

Buhler (2001) indicates "Poor interpersonal skills have been cited as one of the top reasons for managerial failure in the early and middle stages of the management careers." (p.114). this writer brings light to this so that the transitionee has a firm grasp of its importance of the success or failure without this skill.

There are no two people alike that view the world in exactly the same way. The lenses through which they view the world are different-resulting in different perceptions of reality. Effective relationships depend upon understanding these differences.

This writer will leave you, the transitionee, some processes to study and research at another time. They will provide you all the information needed for managing effective relationships within your own organization they will be, (1) The perceptual process, (2) Perception vs. Reality, (3) Perceptual Errors, (4) Attribution, Research and study these four other principles and you will have a complete understanding of the relationship management process.

This writer will highlight what that research study revealed another Critical ingredient in any and all relationships; is trust. The trust of employees generates loyalty and reduces turnover. The trust of customers can generate repeat business. The trust of your creditors can result in credit being extended. Trust also ensures that the company pays their bills on time and maintains their good relationship. Trust, then, is a critical resource to be nurtured in every relationship.

You must build relationships of trust by first extending it. You can't empower a workforce that you do not trust. But you must give people a reason to trust you. Without trust, there is no risk-taken and furthermore, no innovation.

The next issue within this principle of concern is now that you are in management how do you manger your boss a critical relationship which is related to you performance in the organization. However, it is this writers' intension to provide you with certain steps that you can take to ensure that you are effectively managing this most important relationship that with your boss. Consider these suggested skills or tips that follow:

- Invest time to develop the relationship.

- Start to manage your relationship with your boss by knowing yourself, your style, and your own needs.

- View yourself from your boss's perspective.

- Know what your boss expects. You can't meet expectations that you do not know about. Also determine how you performance will be evaluated.

- Observe what your boss does; listen and ask questions to find out what your boss expects.

- Determine how you are going to meet those expectations. Be proactive-don't wait to be told what to do. Take the initiative.

- Support your boss-both privately and publicly. Be loyal, cooperative, and respectful to your superior.

- Find out what interest you and your boss share off the job. This can bring another dimension to the relationship.

- Develop trust. Trust must be mutual, so you must be trustworthy.

- Make sure your boss is always informed. Don't keep secrets.

- Accept criticism. Never become defensive.

- Give credit to your boss. Be instrumental in increasing the visibility of your boss.

- Don't ever expect to get all the praise you need form your boss.

- And lastly do not waste the boss's time. With many demands, you will not be viewed favorably if the time you take is not a good return on investment.

Buhler (2001) indicates that you "should check out the boss you'll be working for before deciding on taken on the position. This relationship can make or break you. Know what you are getting into. If you think you can't work with this individual, do not take the position" (p.123). This writer concurs totally with the fore-mention statement. It literally could be the death of you career and position.

This writer wants to leave this skill set principle with the following general relationships tips. These will enhance your success throughout both your personal life and professional and this writer feels they play a vital role in a successful managerial career.

While there are details to pay attention to in specific relationships you have with various stakeholders, there are general guidelines to keep in mind for all relationships. You must not only be skilled technically, you must also have good human relations skills people must like you. Here are the tips this writer was discussing earlier they are as follows:

- Be positive. Think and act optimistically.

- Smile. This communicates nonverbally that you are approachable.

- Demonstrate concern for others. Be sincere about this concern and be sensitive to others.

- Engage in active listening. Hear people out without interrupting. Draw people out.

- Use empathy. Make an effort to understand the feelings of others. Be open-minded about what you learn.

- Celebrate other's successes.

- Show respect for others. Be polite. Think about what you're doing and the impact of your actions. Avoid hurtful and offensive behaviors.

- Ask for advice and input from others.

- Reserve judgment until you have all the information. Avoid snap judgments.

- Avoid complaining.

- Consider opinions and ideas that are different from your own. Respect other's views. View criticism as an opportunity to make improvements.

- Demonstrate a good sense of humor. You will appear more approachable and likeable. Laugh at yourself.

Buhler (2001, p.126) stated, "Using people's names is a sign of respect. To better remember someone's; repeat it in talking to the person to ingrain it in your memory".

The last of the seven success principles will be on stress. This writer felt it important to include this principle so that the transitionee can get a feel and knowledge of what to be aware of. The potential for stress is every-where. While stress is said to be unavoidable, it is not unmanageable. This writer will try to provide some insights into stress and some tools to better handle and manage stress. For the purpose of this study the focus will be on work related types of stresses.

As you begin your new roles stresses occur to expectations that you have put on yourself, expectations from subordinates, and expectations from your new boss. Interestingly, "nearly 50 percent of American workers per-ceive their jobs to have high level of stress" (Buhler, 2001, p. 300)

- **Stress**—is simply defined as the emotion and physical wear and tear of life. Stress may be thought of as your body's response to life.

The body goes through physiological changes during stress. This is known as the Alarm stage this write intension is to make transitioning pro-fessionals aware of the factors involved in this very critical and important health factor. Not much thought is given to stress when someone is being promoted to more responsible position.

These stress factors will help you understand them and what to watch out for. The following are some physiological responses that may have these conditions:

- Rapid breathing
- Rapid heart beat
- Increased hormone production
- Increased perspiration

- Interrupted digestion
- Tense muscles
- Dilated pupils

With stress, the body is prepared to either fight or run. The adrenaline flow during stress enables one to better handle any dangers that are present.

- Stressors—these are the conditions that trigger stress in people. There are both work and nonwork stressors. And, there are numerous categories or stress within each type.

Different people perceive stressors very differently. And, the person's interpretation of the stressor is the key. It is the way in which you perceive your world that determines how you react to stress. What is stressful for one may not be for the other.

This writer will now attempt to list the key work related stressors that the research revealed they are as follows:

- Task demands
- Role demands
- Interpersonal demands
- Physical demands

- Task demands focus on the job itself. They include change and uncertainly for employees. When people feel they have no control over what they do, they experience stress. Having too many demands, fewer future job opportunities, and new technology introduced can create stress.

- Role demands include role conflict and role ambiguity. Roles involve the expectations that other have on people. Employees may experience conflicting roles—that is, conflicting expectations that cannot be met. Or the organization may expect something of an employee that is not consistent with his or her own values. These ethical dilemmas can create stress. A stressor is experienced when people are not sure what is expected (which is also known as role ambiguity).

- Interpersonal demands reflect stressors related to relationships in the organization. These include dealing with abrasive people (or any conflicting personality type), sexual harassment, and difficult, conflicting leadership styles. Pressures to conform to group norms may also cause stress. If the management style of the manager or supervisor doesn't match the direct subordinate's, stress is also likely to occur.

- Physical demands create stress; and especially when there are unpleasant working conditions on the job (such as unsafe conditions or extreme temperatures), stress cans result. Physical stressors include strenuous activities such as physically demanding work as well as unsatisfactory office conditions, including poor design, poor lighting, no privacy, noise, or even the use of computers.

Another stressor is noise. The sound of human voices has been found to be very distracting. The move to open office plans has increased the noise and distraction levels while decreasing the privacy for its employees.

This writer will discuss basically two personality types so that the transitionee will be able to possibly relate his or her type and to better understand which type they maybe. Again! This writer feels that if you are aware of such traits it will allow you to find a common ground to be less susceptible to stress.

- Personality type A or B—A type "A" personality tends to display what is known as a "coronary-prone behavior" (because they are predisposed to coronary heart disease). They are twice as likely to have coronary heart disease as a type "B". Type A individuals also display a sense of urgency, a focus on achievements, insecurity about status, and are very competitive, impatient, extremely work-oriented, and relentlessly driven.

Type "B"—this type is totally the opposite of "A". These individuals have a weaker sense of time urgency, are less confident, they process a more balanced life, and are more relaxed. Type B's personalities are more contemplative and works at a steady pace. They don't feel as pressured by deadlines as the type A personality. However, interestingly enough, type B individuals are known to be more creative because they are more contemplative.

This writer brings the two types of personalities into the fold so you can determine which personality type you think that you possess if you are a type A. You may want to rethink your habits and become more humorous, become a better manager of your time, and learns not to overextend yourself with too many commitments.

This study will outline the final phases of this principle, entitled organizational consequences of stress. This writer will discuss the prevention of stress management and what the stages are associated with it. Which will be concluded with recognizing stress in others? The concluding and final discussion will be with you as a manager on how you can make a difference.

- Organizational Consequences of stress—If you and your organization fail stress, the following conditions may occur:
  - Low moral
  - High levels of employee dissatisfaction
  - Poor communication
  - Flawed decision-making
  - Poor productivity
  - Poor quality work
  - Increased downtime of equipment
  - Poor relationships with colleagues
  - Work stoppage
  - High accident rates
  - High levels of turnovers
  - High levels of tardiness
  - High levels of absenteeism

Buhler (2001) indicated, "Stress-related claims made by employees against their employers are on the rise. Judgments as high as $1.5 million have been awarded" (p. 305). Research finds transitions to be of sever consequence for both you as a transitionee and to ones organization. The above conditions will allow you to have a better understanding on what to lookout for in your success as a manager.

Belker (1997) says "Much of what seems stressful when you're new in management will seem ordinary and even mundane after you experienced it" (p. 197). Belker (1997) continues with a statement that to succeed, you must convert the fear of the stressful situation into the challenge of a stress situation (p. 198).

This writer will discuss stress management and prevention. There are primarily three stages of prevention. Buhler (2001) indicates these are as follows:

- Stage 1—Primary prevention, by an organization focuses on the elimination or reduction of the source of the stress. Individual prevention focuses on how you can manage stress. This to include such things as optimism, time management, and leisure activities. When you keep a positive outlook, you generally use more humor and laugh more.

- Stage 2—Secondary prevention, involves the modification of the response to the stressor. Team building is a good example. Other secondary prevention can include physical exercise, relaxation training, and diet.

- Stage 3—Tertiary prevention, this prevention is in a form of therapy to heal the symptoms. Organizations provide employee assistance programs for stressors in the work place

These studies will now layout what some of the signs in stress that you can recognize in the work place. This is important mainly due to one thing; work place violence. As a general rule of thumb, you look for changes from whatever is normal for an individual. Buhler (2001) indicates that "there is actually less stress reported by top management levels in an organization than at the lower levels-contrary to what people may initially think. It is thought this may be the result of more control being given to those higher in the organization. Lack of control adds to stress." (p. 308). Some of the signs will be listed below:

- Fatigue and low energy levels
- Inability to concentrate
- Anxiety
- Compulsive eating disorders
- Different work habits
- Moodiness
- Emotional outburst
- Aggression
- Violence
- Depression
- Heart problems

These are a few indicators that you as a manager can recognize. This research has covered a lot of ground on the seven success principles for your transition into management. This writer wanted this dissertation to be a learnard paper that anyone transitioning into management could benefit from and to use to better equip him or her for the transition into management.

This study will now conclude with some guidelines that an effective manager can use to make a difference. There are twelve stressors factors that you can manage.

- Review workloads. Requiring too much out of employees will create stress and ultimately reduce performance levels.

- Eliminate ethical dilemmas where possible. When your employees' values and ethics are more aligned with yours, the possibilities for stress will be minimized.

- Create interesting jobs for employees. Boring, routine jobs often create stress.

- Recognize that stress is different for everyone. Just because a certain condition would not create stress for you, doesn't mean that it is not a major stress for one of your employees. Remember to watch for signs of stress and be open-minded.

- Recognize the fact that there is life (and stressors) out side the work place. Part of being a good manager is helping your employees balance work and nonwork issues.

- Involve employees in change. Uncertainty and the unknowing creates stress. Involving your employees in such will reduce some of the stress.

- Encourage healthier lifestyles. Provide incentives for employees to lose weight or to top smoking.

- Set a good example. Be a good role model for stress prevention.

- Determine the optimal stress levels for each employee. Everyone needs some stress. However, that optimal level will be unique to each individual.

- Learn where the stressors are. Once you are aware of stressors you will be able to change the environment where possible to eliminate.

- Develop a supportive environment. It has been proven that rigid formal environments tend to create more stress then the less formal environment.

- Use career planning. An action plan allows employees to know their next move and thereby may reduce any uncertainties about the future.

Topic Three: Basis for study about transitions

The writer for this study used a study about professionals transitioning into management. As it was the closest study this researcher could find that was similar to the issues at hand within the writers own organization.

Research Description

Hill (2003) had conducted earlier research on the retaining middle managers in financial service firms. In that project she interviewed more than 100 mid-career level managers about their careers and organizations. However, she was struck by the disproportionate attention these managers devoted to the vehemence with which they described their earliest experiences as manager.

She became intrigued by the apparent potency of managers' first experiences on the job and began to explore literature. In her findings at that time she found that the managerial press had countless reports of new manager's incompetence, attrition rates, and burnout. Furthermore, she soon found out that "few systemic or rigorous had been done on the transition to management and that we knew surprisingly little about how managers learned to do their jobs" (p. 337). Moreover, much of that limited research on career transitions treated the transitions as an event rather than a process and usually ignored the more person-centered aspects of the transition-that is, the subjective experience and its social psychological consequences. Latack, (1984) offered this critique:

> First, career transitions as a process, rather than an event, are relatively unexplored...it may be premature to base model building of career transitions on preexisting theory...Further studies might adopt a more exploratory, hypothesis-generating approach aimed at describing and classifying how individuals react to different types of transitions, and what individual and organizational factors contribute to and alleviate stress during the transitions. A second research strategy concerns time as a variable. (p. 317)

Furthermore, Hill (2003) made this statement" If management development initiatives are to truly address the needs of new managers, they must be based on an understanding of how new managers think and feel about the experiences of becoming a manager. This why this writer chose her method of study and the subject matter in which she chose to her study. It is of this writers' belief the same issues that arose from her research will be very similar to this researchers method of research and the out come of the study will hold true within the DOD branch of the Federal Government as well as all internal organizations and divisions. These issues as they are bought to life need to become a way of understanding the transitioning related challenges faced by the technical specialist.

Hill (2003) began to fill this void as she conducted an exploratory field base study of the transition from individual contributor to manager. From a theoretical viewpoint becoming a manager begins when a person is promoted from individual contributor to manager and ends when the when the individual totally understands and masters the managerial role as successfully as he or she can given his or her ability and organizational resources and constraints.

Research Objective

Hill (2003) objective was to describe the experience of becoming a manager from the new manager's point of view with the following questions:

1. What do new managers find most challenging?

2. How do they learn to managers?

3. On what resources, individual and organizational, do they rely? (p. 338).

Although, Hill (2003) interest primarily was driven by a practical agenda, the theoretical implications of such a project-for careers, managerial behaviors, managerial learning, role theory and socialization-seemed self-evident. Hill (2003), Stated, "I was neither testing theory nor seeking to develop theory," (p. 338). However, I hoped to provide a conceptual framework for making sense of the transition to management and to generate a prolific hypothesis for further investigation.

This study is intended to awaken others to further carry out this type of investigation within divisions of government agencies. It is the wish of this writer that transitionee's learn the principles of earlier topics that have been discussed in this paper. And to comprehend and understand what it is and what it takes to be a successful manager.

Methodology Used

Hill (2003) says the phenomenon of interest always dictates the methodology for studying it. Her study was focused on "how" and "why" questions about contemporary events, it seemed that a qualitative field of study was the logical approach. Yin (1984) also discusses exploratory research in that if the form of the questions are of "who", "what", "where", "how" and "why" which will provided the researcher with important clues regarding the most revenant research strategy to be used (p. 22). Hill (2003) as indicated earlier in this text conducted a qualitative field study where she spoke of having formal interviews and relied on observation and informal conversations (in hallways, at meals, during breaks in formal meetings), well-and ill-informants, and archival and published materials.

Hill (2003) periodically would visit and make observations of the newly appointed managers while on their first year on the job. The primary sources of data were semi-structured interviews and unstructured observations. However, as the research progressed and patterns seemed to form, she probed more deeply into the issues that appeared to dominate and to question more precisely and makes more focused observations.

Hill (2003) stated she "interviewed the new managers by phone" (p. 339). She also claimed to her best recollections that her time invested with each participant was approximately twelve days for each. She also included the time spent with the individuals and their senior management, human resource managers, experienced peer managers, and peers in other functional areas. It also includes time spent in selected orientation and training session held for the managers.

The study will incorporate the methods into this study by interviews by phone and creating a descriptive survey and do to the exploratory nature of this research a qualitative study will be devised to account for the main issues for technical advisors transitioning into the management competency.

Approach Sampling Description

Hill (2003) identified five companies——three in the financial service industry and two in the computer industry. Hill (2003) wanted to keep the sample study small no more than ten to twenty managers. There were three reasons for the selection of the companies: (1) was it large enough to have a sizable cohort of new managers for the time period of the investigation would last, (2) were leaders in their respective industries, and (3) did they have a reputation for providing significant opportunities for management training and development and upward mobility?

Studies Results in Summary

The most noteworthy finding by and large was stated by Hill (2003), which said: "Listening to them, it becomes clear that the transition to manager is not limited to acquiring competencies and building relationships. Rather, it constitutes a profound transformation, as individuals learn to think, feel, and value as managers" (Hill, 2003, p. 5).

Some of her findings were related to this research in that she discovered issues as "managing effective relationships with subordinates and their bosses" (Hill, 2003, p. 77). Expectations of the new managers role, authority or delegating, the Chinese fire drill as to were there was too many issues going on, the acknowledgement of having to get things done through others and the skills required to accomplish such tasks, communication, performance, stress, may be found below.

Limitations of the Research

Hill (2003) noted the limitations of relying on self-report identified as the basis of input for personal transformation. However, she also noted that she couldn't think of another way to acquire this type of information. Another, limitation was that the result of the research was not generalized. The contributors of the study were security firm managers (SFMs) and computer company managers (CCMs). Therefore, her study was limited in that it was in a small limited industry. Furthermore, the assumption of her study was more of a typically qualitative interview method: that through the experiences of others an appreciation for conducting interviews and observations could become better understood from those methods.

Future Research Issues

Hill (2003) suggested further research on managers in various functions in the discussion of the study.

Studies Significance

Hill's (2003) study identified critical issues in transition from a contributor to manager. While her objectives of the study were larger in range, they sided with this research. Hills ability was of value when she made a comparison point for the data analysis phase of her research. Hill identified categories that were than compared with those extracted from the conducted interviews of her study, providing the strength and support for the validity of the studies findings.

Chapter 2 Summary

The writer reviewed literature that related to the transitions of professional individuals to manager as discussed per Hill (2003) studies. Due to the context of the study there was a lack of literature available on what technologist or professional individuals experienced and what the challenges were in the transition to manager especially in the technical specialist realm of the Federal Government.

The review of literature in this chapter was separated into three topics. In the first topic, a brief history was given on the three most well known theories for an insight of the fundaments of management. Topic two discussed the essential skills needed for the transition to management as this writer's research found seven principles that seem to be the talking points throughout all the research material studied.

This writer wanted to give a learnerd type of paper so anyone could become aware of what the skills would be in becoming a successful manager. And who ever may read this paper may wish to continue with such studies in other branches of the government or in the private sector as well. This writer in topic two discussed the functions of management and the four areas of them, which were Planning, Organizing, Controlling and Leading.

This researcher after reading numerous books and text in trade articles carefully listed the seven success principles that seemed to be of the most talked about and written about. This writer wanted the transitionee to have all the skills that seemed to be needed for a smoother transition, and made them aware of what it would encompass to become a successful manager. Those skills were communication, conflicts, delegating, motivation, performance, and relationships and concluded with stress. Topic three discussed the basis for the study as Hill (2003) conducted a similar study about the transition to management in the financial and computer industries. Her studies provided support for promoting professionals and technologist into management and formed the basis for the method and questioning of this study.

Chapter 3
Methodology

Approach

The approached used for this study is comprised of an exploratory method with a qualitative technique of interviewing for the ranking of the study's results. A descriptive survey was developed and conducted via interviews to determine what the technical specialist felt to be the most challenging and key issues of their transition.

This researcher is a technical specialist with over 20 years experience in this related field with the D.O.D. The past eight years has been served as a weapons systems specialist. The researcher of this paper attempted to transition into management and upon doing so encountered resistance. It became clearer that once you are highly competent in your chosen field opposition to promotion was obvious due to the fact that the task you were assigned to could not be filled.

From this personal experience this writer felt compelled to conduct a study on those who had made the transition successfully. Once these issues are brought to life the possibility of a much less rigid thought maybe applied and not hinder those is a specialty field.

Exploratory Research

Exploration is particularly useful when researchers lack a clear idea of the problems they will meet during the study. This method of study serves other purposes as well. In the area of investigation may be so new or so vague that a researcher needs to do an exploration study just to learn something about the dilemma facing new managers. Such was the case with this research; any other technical specialist has never addressed this type of study. The technical specialist accepted the fact that once they were highly competent they would remain stuck and topped out at their present level. This was the case of this researcher and that is why this topic was chosen for the research study.

Qualitative Techniques

Objectives of exploration research may be accomplished with different techniques. Both qualitative and quantitative techniques are applicable, although exploration relies more heavily on qualitative techniques. The following are some considerations of determining the scope of qualitative research. This writer will list those of which were the deciding factors for this study:

1. In-depth interviewing (usually conversational rather than structured).

2. Participant observations (to perceive firsthand what participants in the setting experience).

3. Case studies (for an in-depth contextual analysis of a few events or conditions).

4. Proxemics and kinesics (to study the use of space and body-motion communication, respectively). This chapter will discuss the methodology used in the study. (Cooper & Schindler, 2003, p. 152)

By using the aforementioned approaches an experience survey can emerge. Thus, given ones organization a proprietary in sight to its own internal issues. When interviewing persons in this style of survey, we seek ideas about important issues or aspects of the subject matter and discover what the importance is across the range of the knowledge.

Descriptive Study

In contrast to exploratory studies "more formalized studies are typically structured with clearly stated investigative questions" (Cooper & Schindler, 2003, p. 161). Formal studies serve a variety of research objectives:

1.   Descriptions of phenomena or characteristics associated with subject population (who, what, when, where, and how of a topic).

This study will devise a formal questionnaire and once answered the qualitative data will be collected and broken into the top four issues that arose from the survey.

Reasoning for the methods chosen

The reason these three methods of study were chosen was that they played a part in the formulation for the rationale of the study. This writer lacks what the issues were and what problems may occur during the study that explains the exploratory research. The qualitative technique was established though the method of conversational interviewing rather than a more structured format in the beginning of the research. Finally, the descriptive study was used for a more formal structured questionnaire so that a tabulation could be comprised that would enable this writer to determine the main issues or topics of concerns from the study.

One of the main reasons for this research was to discover the phenomena of the common experience of the technical specialist transitioning into program management this type of research can uncover common and shared experiences.

The interviewing technique used was to acquire and record the experiences of the interviewee's transition into management. Moustakas (1994) indicates that phenomenon describes the meaning of experiences for several individuals on a topic or concept. This writer found this to be the case while conducting the transitions from a technical competency to a management competency.

Data Gathering Method

The gathering of data was comprised of the three methods of study listed at the beginning of chapter 3. The two criteria's for the survey, first this writer used Hill (2003) to form the basis of this study as she used qualitative methods. Second the descriptive survey method was used to gather the information of a formative format and upon the completion of this questionnaire this research was able to complete and address the top issues that the transitionee's faced.

This study could also include phenomenology as it was from the shared experiences of the transitionee's and the core of the mutual understanding of the experience.

Database of Study

Hill (2003) was used to base the transitions into management by her survey methods were it was intended that the managers had been in their roles long enough to comment on their experiences about their transitions. She determined that a year was long enough for her contributors to have experienced the wide range of experiences during the first year of their promotion. She also suggested that managers took on average three years feel that they were in control of their new roles as manager.

This criterion was one part of the qualitative research method she used as she placed a 1–5 year limitation on that area of topic. After a data analysis was performed it demonstrated significant redundancy. It was also noted that the transition was long. She explains this as the contributor was acting as a manager without the formal job title as manager.

The second part was of this writer formal survey being descriptive in nature once these questions were completed a point value was given and the top four were then addressed as the most challenging aspects of their transition.

Validity of Data

The use of the methods describe throughout this paper will allow the transitionee to grasp and visualize the transitioning challenges faced by technical specialist into the program management field within the Department of Defense within the weapons branch of the Federal Government. By conducting the descriptive formal survey through exploratory means and comprising them into a ranking of a qualitative technique will emerge a scheme of the most important issues in the transition. Therefore, allowing individuals to become better prepared for their own transition and acquiring the skills necessary and the patience necessary to handle the transition. This research will be able to identify those issues and rank them in accordance to the most important. As stated earlier by detecting these issues the transitionee can better prepare himself or herself for the transition and to better understand the expectations anticipated from themselves and others.

Originality and Limitations of Data

The research of this study is limited in ways that are very common in a qualitative research study mainly in the fact that they are normally generalized to the normal population. This study focused a certain part of the phenomenon of transition into management. Therefore, implying that it is not expected to accurately represent the overall spirit of the transition due to the portion the research questions were focused on. The entire technical specialists in this study were male. And very limited as their have only been five TS who have made that transition successfully.

This study focused on the challenges faced by TS as they were promoted into a management competency. And what were the main issues and concerns during their transitions. Once these issues and concerns are addressed a smoother and a more fair structure can be looked at for the promotion of TS. The survey was structured in a way for interviewing so that it would highlight issues in the pursuant search for growth in a technical competency to a management one.

Summary of Chapter 3

This chapter discusses the methods of this research. The approach used with the three methods containing the exploratory, qualitative, and descriptive where each was explained why they were chosen. Followed by the data gathering method were Hill (2003) was chosen for her studies as a basis. Then a descriptive questionnaire was developed to help isolate what the challenges were for the transitionee's and the phenomena of such a transition. These then lead to the database of study where Hills (2003) thoughts were applied to this study. The validity of the data gathered was through the techniques described within this paper. One contributing factor was a qualitative technique being used to formulate a quantities result and then apply those findings in a ranking structure of what the most challenges and skills needed for the transition.

The originality came from this writer's inability to make a successful transition and was seeking out those who had. By this writers ability to search out and conduct these interviews to the very selected few gave a better understanding to the process and skills needed for such a transition. And what the challenges and obstacles they faced along the way. It further gave an average number of years it took for trying on the participant's behalf to transition. The issue was that there were limited specialist in the weapons who made the transition and it was never looked at the division level. And the disparity of such promotions to other organizations structures as it related to TS in the weapons branch and the success rates of each.

Chapter 4

Data Analysis

Overview

The main focus of this study was to increase the understanding and to learn from the challenges that the TS's faced in their transition from a technical competency to a management competency and once promoted into the new competency the skill sets required for that transition. The data will show what the new awakening was into that management field and will try to better prepare future transitionee's in what skills are conducive for a smoother and a successful transition. Figure 1 will show the process and the data flow used in gathering and preparing the data in this chapter. This chapter uses the methods described in chapter 3 for the data gathering and analysis. The collection of data via the interview process will be the PM's experiences as identified in the questioner then once identified will then be presented back to the managers who will validate them and rank them accordingly. As a result the four most main areas of discussion were to be considered the most important by the interviewees in the aspects of the transitioning into the management competency. Ranked in order of the most important key issues and skills needed to becoming an effective manager. There were six initial questions presented to the five participants in the descriptive interview. An exploratory approach was chosen with an objective by using a qualitative method and was the main focus on finding the very nature of technical specialist transitions into a program manager's position.

A descriptive survey was developed that encompassed the following six questions. They were formulated for this study so that a better understanding and knowledge could be gained and acquired about the transition. Then in turn future technical specialists would be better equipped and prepared themselves when they are considered a new transitionee. After examining the study group's transition a very unique insightfulness will emerge.

1. How their technical expertise were related to a managerial related context during the transition form a TS to a PM?

2. Are the management aspects of the position more challenging then first thought, once appointed to management was there a career developmental program?

3. Were there any certifications that needed to be completed and if so what was the process like?

4. What did they like while being a TS and now as a Pm, and the same for their dislikes on both positions?

5. How were and if any individual and organizational resources do they rely on and were there any commonality between being a technical specialist and a program manager?

6. How difficult were and what were the main issues in the transition from a TS to PM?

The research questions will be presented to each of the five interviewees followed by their answers. After the conclusion of the interviewee's answers, tabulation will be comprised. With the most challenging in the transition of which the top four issues being presented as the abstract of this researches works revealed.

1. Expectations of the position.

2. Abundance of issues.

3. Affiliation changes.

4. Allocating

The conclusion of this chapter will reveal the results and will be ranked in order of difficulty.

Brief Overview of Procedures

The interviewees were technical specialist that held a professional degree in engineering and now holds a program managers position in the federal government of the department of defense. There locations were Pax River, Maryland, Pt. Mugu, California and China Lake, California.

The interviewees were asked to participate in this study and signed a consent form. Even though it is a relatively small pool this researcher knew all the participants. Interviews were conducted via email or by a phone call. After these interviews were complete a case analysis was prepared once all interviews were accomplished the managers were ask to rank them according to difficulty.

As stated earlier the overall objective was to get a better understanding of the transition from a technical specialist to a program manager with the department of defense in the federal government. Those questions were indicated on the onset of this chapter.

In presenting the data some extensive quotes are used as reported by the managers. Creswell's (1998) recommends that the interviewees be allowed to speak for themselves.

The following sections are the case studies for each of the interviewees. These studies will establish some background and a perspective of the experiences and challenges the interviewees faced in their transition. The areas of discussion include: technical expertise related to managerial context during the transition; was the managerial more challenging then first thought; was a training developmental program available to assist in the new role; if there were certifications required for their new position and if so what was that like; what did they like and dislike about both; were there any organizational resources that they rely on and was there any commonality; what comments were made and seemed to be the main issues in the transition.

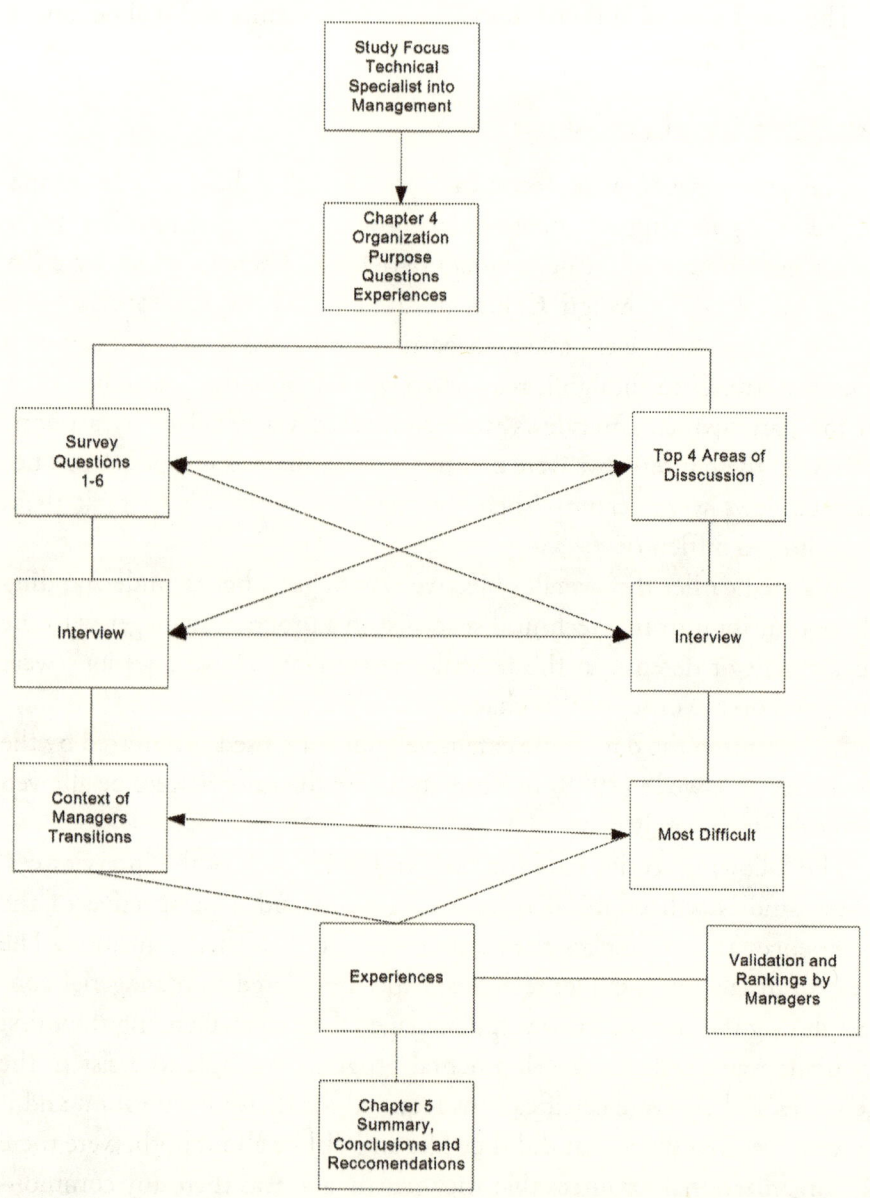

Figure 1. Process model for analysis and chapter 4

Survey Questions and Responses of the Interviewee's

Walt

The following interview will discuss Walt's comments relative to the research survey questioner.

Question 1:

How their technical expertise were related to a managerial related context during the transition form a TS to a PM?

One of the most difficult adjustments that I made from a technical field into a management one was the constant changing of new tasks and not having the ability to concentrate on one thing or being able to see a specific assignment into it's conclusion:

- "This was a one of the dislikes I had for being a manager"

- "My concern is that there were to many issues going on at the same time...he always was in a state of feeling like a target always on foot moving about...trying to keep ahead of the game by coordinating efforts so they the project would not crash."

Question 2:

Are the management aspects of the position more challenging then first thought, once appointed to management was there a career developmental program?

- "I experienced much more responsibility"

- "My stress level also increased"

- "Due to deadlines such as milestones, budgets and top level pressures from above...upon coming home I would totally be all stressed out due to the fact I knew I had to get a lot of things done at work."

Question 3:

Were there any certifications that needed to be completed and if so what was the process like?

- "I had to complete an intense DIAWA training program within 18 months I was learning a whole new language and terms for my new position. The level 3 certification was just daunting…the level 1 was fairly easy and informative…level 2 is where the fun began and my mind was on overload."

- "The process seemed to be intense at least for me as I really could not relate to what was being said or taught…It seemed to be a cram session of information."

- "The process took me the entire 18 months, as I had to also to continue with my new position kind-a-learn as you go mentality."

- "I now have to complete 80 hours of continuous learning to keep certified another pressure".

Question 4:

What did they like while being a TS and now as a PM, and the same for their dislikes on both positions?

- "My likes about being a technical specialist were…my freedom to create…the ability to solve a problem…the ability to take the ownership in that I did that…being able to remain focused on a single task…seeing that 100% of your time was getting it correct and right the first time…seeing the final result of your actions."

- "My dislikes about being a technical specialist were…I could not control my fate…other supervisors or managers telling me what to do and when to have it done by."

- "If a project was to be preformed by a group I could not control the whole projects outcome…therefore if another individual's portion was not quite up to par it reflected on the entire project."

- "My career became very limited…growth potential was nil…management was the only true way for growth and promotion."

- "My likes about being a manager are…I enjoy having more responsibility…I have been able to obtain a broader knowledge and my overall product knowledge has increased and my ability to understanding the total process involved from the inception to completion and why we have safe guards in place and understanding total life cycle cost of an new developmental program."

- "One of my biggest likes about being a manager is that I am viewed more as an expert now and others seek out my opinion."

- "My dislikes about being a manager is…I cannot focus on multiple tasks nor do I have the ability to follow something through to its completed cycle."

- "My target goals are only set for a 90% rate in solving problems instead of 100%…I am not seen as one of the guy any longer. I am now at times considered the adversary…the other guy…not one of them…the enemy."

- "I no longer have the friendships that I once had…I do not have the creativity to solve problems on a technical aspect of things."

- "My total ownership of accomplishing a task and seeing it through…I find myself not able to control things as much as I hoped…mainly due to the demands put forth by upper management and their strategy always takes precedence."

- "I will also like to include with my opinion about the transition in this section. My likes about making the transition are…having the opportunity to do it…I always aspired to become a manager but never thought it would happen, as it is very rare."

- "I was surprised about the fact how hard it was to transition into such a role…it was much harder then expected…I really enjoy the overall project results, but not necessary the processes you had to go through to get it done."

- "I liked be given more responsibility…I saw myself singled out from others doing the same management functions…I now have the upward mobility I always wanted within the department of defense in the federal government."

Question 5:

How were and if any individual and organizational resources do they rely on and were there any commonality between being a technical specialist and a program manager?

- "Well I tried to have someone mentor me...that was about the only individual resource I had...the DIAWA program was developed as a tool to acquire certain skill sets required for a program manager's position."

- "As for commonality's the two competencies are miles apart...I wish that there were skill sets available while in a technical field to allow you to better prepare for a management field within the federal government."

- "I realized early on after my appointment to my new position that I needed better people skills...better communication skills...administrative skills I hardly ever gave presentations or ran a meeting or prepared an agenda before."

- "I found motivating employees was difficult...just to interact with people was challenging...in meetings trying to keep organized and in line with the meetings topic and not getting side tracked."

- "Learning to deal with getting resources...staffing issues...and any other means to accomplish the task at hand was difficult as a technical specialist I did not have these issues so there isn't any commonality between the two."

Question 6:

How difficult was it and what were the main issues in the transition from TS to PM?

Walt indicated several other issues associated with the transition, they were that he was now perceived on a different plane and consider not being 'one of guys', he now was thought of not as a friend but a foe.

- "As a technical specialist we worked for one person and for the most part equal...However after the transition I at times was not an equal...sometimes although rare I was, and most of the time I was now considered to be the adversary, the enemy not one of them."

- "I would feel some resentment from individuals saying things like well, Walt is at the helm now he's the man in charge, and don't you know. They then would state something to the effect like that they should be in charge."

- Walt thought "he would gain instant respect right away when he was put in charge and being I was on of them they would want to do a good job for me. And that wasn't the case at all.... I have no idea what ever gave me that impression."

- "My biggest issue was allocating tasks I was always doing and completing task on my own…but now I struggled with the fact I wasn't able to do so and…as a technical specialist I could personally accomplish it…if it was a dead line I would call home and tell the wife I had to finish the project and I wasn't coming home till I was done…Now I cannot do that as a manager…because they are now the responsibility of someone else."

- Another problem "I felt was I had to rely heavily on other people to get thing done and now being held accountable for others peoples work."

- "I liked my technical aspect of my job before the transition, the accomplishment of finishing an assignment from start to end. I started with my own hands and saw the completed product at the end…and you knew it was due to your efforts. As a manager the hands on approach was no longer the way…By me allocating the task I felt no longer as a contributor. And that upset me like nothing else."

- Allocating what "I wanted done in a design for example just did not work…I now had to experience a teaming of ideas allowing the individual assigned to the task the ability to work it in his or her way. It was a hard pill to swallow not being able to still not getting the task done the way I wanted it done I had a particular way in my head…however I now have learned my lesson on allocating."

- "I came to grip with that these things are not under my control and all I can do is to do my best in meeting them."

Dave

The following interview will discuss Dave's comments relative to the research survey questioner.

Question 1:

How their technical expertise were related to a managerial related context during the transition form a TS to a PM?

- "My technical expertise was to no avail...once promoted being a mechanical engineer...I had not a clue when I was the program manager for software integration."

- "I had to learn how to manage outside my comfort zone of technical knowledge."

- "I was not prepared for all that a manager would need as for skill sets...as a TS I worked with others of the same background and was tasked with one focus...as for the management side of things I was bombarded with issues, funding, man power ect. There was no relation to have...except I have been with the government for 20 plus years."

Question 2:

Are the management aspects of the position more challenging then first thought, once appointed to management was there a career developmental program?

- "Much longer hours...the development and learning via difficult times as you are growing into the newly appointed position."

- "The competitions...the ways others will back stab you to get to the top."

- "No one was there to help guide you through the ruff times the deep black hole you often fell in...when others could have help you avoid them."

- "How often when things are good...and then bam something comes from nowhere to knock you down a peg or two."

- "Over coming the perception that I did not know what I was doing...all the above mention statements I viewed to be challenging in the transition role of accepting the position and once there wow."
- "Yes, there is a DIAWA program in which you get 18 months to complete to become a fully certified level 3 program manager...of which you had to arrange for yourself."
- "As a program manager I am making hundreds of thousand dollars decisions a day sometimes millions...as a technical specialist maybe I made a few hundred dollar decisions in a day."
- "It is all about budgets and keeping them with the scope of the project and on time a major challenge."
- "In order to be considering a productive manager...you had to hit your milestones...because you were being judged by what other had accomplished before you a challenge."

Question 3:

Were there any certifications that needed to be completed and if so what was the process like?

- "I was tasked to complete a level 3-certification process within 18 months of my appointment to program manager and do my job as well."
- "The course work and classes were of mind boggling proportions, way too much information to comprehend in the period of time allocated on top of everything else"
- "I was not prepared for such information overload."

Question 4:

What did they like while being a TS and now as a PM, and the same for their dislikes on both positions?

- "I liked being a technical specialist simply for the fact I could solve problems."

- "I seemed to always be creating or designing something I liked that."

- "My sense of seeing a final product and achieving the accomplishment of the project...it was the hands on approach I was able to take."

- "I really enjoyed working as a team as equals on the same playing field."

- "My dislike about being a TS was when management set goals and deadlines that were way out reach...always felt as though management never."

- "I disliked the fact it seemed that there was no end to the workload, to keep on top of the task being assigned...the pressure was at times just unbearable."

- "My likes for management...I enjoy having the ability to manage a project...the interactions with the individuals and building relationships."

- "I find my knowledge increase on more business issues and I am intrigued by that...I like earning the respect of my department and them knowing you are a good leader."

- "I like to motivate...the people working for me."

- "I know it was a step forward in my career"

- "My dislikes about being a manager...losing the technical skills hat I so long honed over the years...I am not able to touch and feel any longer."

- "I have to come in on or under budget a tremendous pressure and dislike...many times I have to be the middleman individuals and upper management."

- "I find it if your employees like you...you will be fine if not stand by."

- "I don't like being treated by upper management as if I haven't grown into my position...and them not sharing more information with me."

- "Another big dislike is I was once considered an expert in my department...and now not anymore."

- "A hurdle and a big dislike is the fact most upper managers do not feel they have to work with you...and God forbid you make a suggestion that is out side the box of their thinking."

- "Upper management always takes the credit for the good things that happen...but you are the first to blame if something goes wrong."

- "It seems that everything upper management does reflects on you excellent job or decision or a poor job or decision on their part...to many areas of responsibilities."

- "A dislike the interruptions throughout the day...which in turns take me away from my assigned duties...always seems I am making tradeoffs or compromises."

- "I dislike working longer hours to get things done...and not getting compensated for it."

Question 5:

How and if any individual and organizational resources do they rely on and were there any commonality between being a technical specialist and a program manager?

- "In my case not many resources...as for commonality...I was in for an eye waking experience...the skills needed to become an effective leader/manager...I was just a pup in this arena."

- "My communication skills, lacked...the how to motivate your subordinates work and excite them about their work...and making them do it."

- "Resolving issues or conflicts...performance...handling stress."

- "The building of relationships...being able to talk with individuals...the time you must spend in getting to know personalities."

- "I wasn't aware of how many people skills were required and all of the different situations that occur in that realm alone."

- "How much more overtime was required being a manager...of which I am not happy at this stage of my life."

- "I was expected to pull resources out of the hat...now being a manager I was held accountable for everything."

- "The balancing of responsibilities was way different then first thought...I also did not have the power or the authority over my programs, as I was lead to believe especially in the beginning of my promotion."

- "I felt like a novice...I had a ton to learn as a new manager...I found that mentoring just wasn't offered and would have been of great help."

Question 6:

How difficult were and what were the main issues in the transition from a TS to PM?

- "One of my biggest issues was once you become management it seemed...that technical specialist now had a trust issue with me...as before as one of them there weren't any trust issues."

- "I began to feel jealousy from them...you would hear things as...why is Dave there and I am not."

- "My friends now that I was a manager tend to try at least to take advantage of the fact...and when this occurs I have to cut them off."

- "Another issue for me was being careful not to speak ill of a technical specialist...because if you say something about him/her that individual may think you talk about them to someone else."

- "For me performance evolutions were a difficult task...especially when you have known the individuals for quite sometime...now I must evaluate their job performance an uneasy feeling when you must document everything."

- Allocating work was an issue…"I felt it easier the further down the line I was assigning task to."

- A wake up call for me was that "I realized that I had to let go of the technical side of things and now perform in a managers function…the only way to become a good manager in my eyes was to let the technical go."

Bill

The following interview will discuss Bill's comments relative to the research survey questioner.

Question 1:

How their technical expertise were related to a managerial related context during the transition form a TS to a PM?

- "I was promoted into management and instead of leading an electrical engineering department in the technical specialist group…I was put into a field I could not relate to…I knew nothing about it…I felt extremely out of place."

- "I have thought many times I made the wrong decision…accepting the new position…my wife says I am a nerdy kinda of guy who always likes to tinker…and she's right…I just can not do that anymore."

- "I considered this as a significant event in my career…and how my relationships would with my fellow co-workers would be effected by the move into management."

Question 2:

Are the management aspects of the position more challenging then first thought, once appointed to management was there a career developmental program?

- "I had a challenging time trying to deal with the pressures and stress associated with the new position."

- "I did not think of all the problems that I would have to resolve…managing people…conflicts between employees…I sure could have used some training in that area."

- "I now could see a management point of view…as when I was a technical specialist…my own opinion was get rid of management and all troubles would go away…now being in the so called inner circle I can see clearly most of the managers are out of touch with their workers."

- "My being a new guy on the block, I had to soft shoe around…I found you just could not refute anyone…so I felt submissive…and felt that me being a new guy…I was just being brushed aside anyway."

- "I could not stand the office politics…how everyone was looking on how to impress the boss…even if it was at the expense of another manager."

- "It was hard for me to get involved in the corporate game of climbing up the ladder to succeed."

- "Ethic's came into play when I became a manager…so you must deal in an ethical manner."

Question 3:

Were there any certifications that needed to be completed and if so what was the process like?

- "Yes, as with most government management programs…I had to attend the DIAWA classes…I had to become a level 3 certified within an 18-month time frame as per D.O.D instructions."

- "The process that I experienced was grueling and a head exploding ordeal a lot of facets of logistics and everyone's part in the big picture…total stress."

Question 4:

What did they like while being a TS and now as a PM, and the same for their dislikes on both positions?

- "I liked being TS for the bench testing that was being developed for weapon systems."

- "I especially enjoyed being able to troubleshoot and fault isolate software problems that were related to code and debugging as such…just good ole problem solving."

- "I liked the fact I was able to work with the latest equipment in the laboratory testing facility…I had total possession of the element in question and a whole lot a responsibility for getting it done."

- "My dislikes of being a technical specialist was the reporting and the continuous updates needed."

- "As for my likes as being a manager…is primarily the negation between contractors and the government a win/win for both parties."

- "My dislike about being a manager is…the performance evaluation process and all the HR facets associated with it…and the time spent in meetings upon meetings with any resolution in sight…a waste of time."

- "I liked the transition phase…in the fact I was more involved in the decision making process…and it seemed my opinion counted."

- "I also now know more of what is going on."

Question 5:

How and if any individual and organizational resources do they rely on and were there any commonality between being a technical specialist and a program manager?

- "I did not experience any mentoring or any other sort of help in the transition."

- "I now was working 11–12 hours days…when I was a technical specialist I would go home at my normal time."

- "No, there wasn't any commonality…it seemed at least when I was a technical specialist…people were will to help and stay until the task was done…in management it was all about self reliance."

- "I remember upper management saying…'This is the way we do it here' I had to learn everything on my own…It was just a challenge trying to get to the same level of knowledge as the rest."

- "I use to use the term being thrown to the sharks…when it came to facing the seasoned vets of the program management field…they knew who to get answers from and who and where to contact them…when I would ask for help they were always busy."

Question 6:

How difficult were and what were the main issues in the transition from a TS to PM?

- "On of my issues about the transition was how my relationship changed with the technical specialist."

- "In my case it was difficult for me not being able to say I was one of the guy's…because in reality I wasn't a technical specialist…I was now in management."

- "When I received my new promotion…my friends now continued to ask questions…hinting for insider information or you always had something to hide…now I am in a position, which I have privilege information that I did not have privy hadn't before my promotion…I now have to be very careful how I use that information."

- "One of my biggest concerns was performance evaluations…and having to tell my former coworkers how they were ranked for the reporting period."

- "Allocating and trying to manage and organize tasks and control all the aspects of those tasks…that were a difficult transition from TS to a PM."

- "I found myself always wanting to do the task my self…but you know that you are no longer able to do so."

- "I experienced things much differently then first thought…the pressure and stress…many sleepless nights."

Chris

The following interview will discuss Chris's comments relative to the research survey questioner.

Question 1:

How their technical expertise were related to a managerial related context during the transition form a TS to a PM?

- "As a manager I now wasn't viewed as the specialist but as now being the single point of contact...I had to know everything...and when I was a technical specialist I was with my peers and did not feel so inadequate at times...as I did while being in management...not much related context there."

Question 2:

Are the management aspects of the position more challenging then first thought, once appointed to management was there a career developmental program?

- "Yes, the responsibility I felt was much larger...then when I was a technical specialist...I had always felt as I was personally held accountable for my productivity...but now the project is much larger."

- "The pressure...a tremendous amount of more pressures...the stress and pressure of keeping everything moving into the right course of completion."

Question 3:

Were there any certifications that needed to be completed and if so what was the process like?

- "Of course the government has what they call DIAWA certification and as a program manager you must obtain a level 3...that is a mandatory requirement, and it must be completed within 18 months."

- "It was a deluge of information and to a layman such as myself...it was over tasking...relentless on information over load."

- "I had to arrange such course requirement completion on my own and continue to perform my position as well."

Question 4:

What did they like while being a TS and now as a Pm, and the same for their dislikes on both positions?

- "One of the main things I liked about being a technical specialist was I was considered the expert...the one everyone went to."

- "My one major dislike about being a technical specialist was...I did not get to see the big picture or was I involved in the discussions of such a project."

- "One of my main things for liking my manager's role...was that I like the involvement participation at the higher levels.'

- "I also do not miss being a technical specialist...I enjoy rubbing elbows with higher-level managers...and the interactions I have with them."

- "However one thing I dislike about being a manger is the way I must come across to my once co-workers...I come off as firm."

Question 5:

How and if any individual and organizational resources do they rely on and were there any commonality between being a technical specialist and a program manager?

- "As for commonalities...I was working very...I mean...very long hour as a manager...as a technical specialist it was a 7:00 am to 4:00pm job."

- "I found myself doing more work...then allocating the work out to others to do.'

- "I found myself always having to fight for upper management's time and...having them giving me what I needed to accomplish the task at hand."

Question 6:

How difficult were and what were the main issues in the transition from a TS to PM?

- "It was difficult transition…technical specialist being you peers…now they are your subordinates…it was hard one minute you were on their level and now you aren't."

- "The above statement was probably the most difficult and challenging issue for me."

- "I found it very tough to discipline a former peer…I often found them…my formal peers trying to take advantage of me…and our friendship to a point that some of them acted improperly and I was forced to use disciplinary actions…it felt strange for me…it wasn't in my nature to act that way."

- "I found myself always worrying about receiving the respect you should get when you acquire such a title…it always felt I had to prove myself over and over."

- "Being responsible for everyone's work…my biggest challenge was the ability to manage and not doing the work myself…I found myself realizing you can not work and perform a management role effectively…if you are going to manage…you must manage."

- "I found myself wanting to revert back to more of a technical role."

- "I was working enormously long hours."

Joe

The following interview will discuss Joe's comments relative to the research survey questioner.

Question 1:

How their technical expertise were related to a managerial related context during the transition form a TS to a PM?

- "My expertise had no relation to the management side of things…I could have used a lot of training in other skill sets…such as people…motivation and many others…I would have been much better off if I acquired these type of skills before accepting the job."

- "My only thing I could really use was my organizational skills that…helped me the most…everything else as a big learns as you go."

Question 2:

Are the management aspects of the position more challenging then first thought, once appointed to management was there a career developmental program?

- "Oh yeah…the hours…the stress…the people problems the more people it seemed the problems you have."

- "Every time a new project comes your way…or managing several projects at a time…more and more stress…and that's something neither my family nor I like."

- "Just my lack of skills required in the management field in general…communicating…allocating…conflicts…relationships…just to name a few."

- "Everything I knew was of a technical nature…management acumen has it's own skill set."

- "The use of the latest office tools required for the project…and knowing how to use such tools…as a manager you were expected to know those things."

Question 3:

Were there any certifications that needed to be completed and if so what was the process like?

- "I had to attend DIAWA training and achieve a level 3 certification within an 18 moth time frame…again not having any back ground in such issues it was just information going in one ear and out the other."

- "I personally don't know of anyone who had an easy time with the certification process."

Question 4:

What did they like while being a TS and now as a Pm, and the same for their dislikes on both positions?

- "What I like best of being a technical specialist was my freedom and independence…I had complete job liberty as I was a sole sighted specialist away from the main headquarters."

- "I had full rein of problem solving…I could focus on it and solve it…in my own way and time."

- "I could just look at technical issues at my own leisure."

- "My biggest dislike about being a technical specialist was when I had to deal with management…and always be on some type of time table that they though I should be on…the lack of support on being able to do the job."

- "My likes about being a manager…I now have a deeper appreciation for the business side of things."

- "I have a much wider range of knowledge on the overall picture…I better understand company financial records and their importance."

- "I very much enjoy being able to bring my division or group together so they receive the kudos they deserve."

- "I feel as though I am more of a contributor…I feel more valuable to the division and to the organization as a whole."

- "My dislikes about being a manager…having to sometimes still play both roles…as a technical specialist and as a manager…when I am assigned a technical task…I am not always able to complete it in a timely manner…and I know that it is hurting the entire work effort of the team."

Question 5:

How and if any individual and organizational resources do they rely on and were there any commonality between being a technical specialist and a program manager?

- "Commonalities no…when I was a technical specialist…everyone was willing to help each other out…when I became a manager no one wanted to help you out."

- "Being the new guy on the floor…I knew I had to learn from someone and gain the knowledge needed from others…as I did not hold a business degree…I was a technical guy…I was a little fortunate as I had a little from other managers…however it was limited."

Question 6:

How difficult were and what were the main issues in the transition from a TS to PM?

- "A main issue was in the form of relationships…people I have known for years…stated that Joe has gone to the other side…the dark side…the enemy."

- "A trust issue arose with my new appointment into management…everyone was hush…hush not as open with me as they were when I was a technical specialist."

- "I felt that jealously came into play…some individuals now resented me…and were saying things like…why did he get picked over me or someone else and why wasn't it me?"

- "I found myself battling when I had to take disciplinary actions against one of my formal co-workers."

- "My credibility…once I let go of the technical things…I was the go to guy…now I am the guy people curse on why you haven't completed the assignment yet."

- "Allocating…I never dealt with before now…I was always doing it myself…I now have to give it to someone else to do…I have to learn to trust the individual that I assign the task to; as well I wasn't use to any of that."

- "I often feel as I am setting myself up for failure by trusting someone else…as a manager you do not have the time to review in detail the task that needed to be done."

- "Sometimes…I find myself wanting to do what I was comfortable with and that was troubleshooting software issues."

Summary of the Questioner

The very onset of this paper was to explore the need for this type of research, as it has never been addressed before. Would this research benefit the organization as well as being warranted in and of itself? Would this be of interest to the current technical specialist who may be considering the transition?

After conducting an exploratory type of research and feeling a sense of urgency with this topic. This writer began reaching out to other technical specialist and feeling their excitement about this research it was immediately apparent the interest was there. Being this writer's organization is very small in scale only 28 in the division. And at the moment there have only been 5 technical specialists that have made the transition successfully.

I contact the 5 successful former technical specialists and asked them if they would participate in this study. Upon their un-resounded agreement to participate in this survey and as they expressed a very high interest in contributing to and seeing the results in the research collected. They began making comments that they wished that they had some type of insight when it came to their career decision process. I then immediately created a consent form and prepared a descriptive survey that furnished the six most right to the point questions posed for the transition process to the interviewees.

After receiving and collecting the data this researcher had more than 160 responses to the main subject matter as it related to the transitioning from a technical competency to a management competency and qualitative technique could be applied on comprising the most concerning issues or area of discussions. To the surprise of this research this writer was astonished to learn how once you achieved such a status of being promoted into the management field how reluctant the other managers were on helping out the new appointees.

However, it did not surprise this writer of the lack of preparedness and the lack of knowledge about the skill sets needed for such a transition.

Every one of the managers lacked the most in management skills of func-
tionality and their DIAWA training was totally exhausted. The final section of this chapter will be the ranking of the most areas of discussion and
concerns. The interviewees, once this writer collected all the data were in
receipt of the responses from all the contributors and then were asked to
rank them in order of importance.

This writer choose a ranking scale that would be a rating of one to six
one being of extreme importance and six being of least importance. This
research then annotated the main for areas as the most important issues of
the survey.

Observations from the Researcher

The following will include the most challenging observations of this
writer's interpretation of the remarks made by each of the interviewees.
This then will be followed by the ranking of each of the issues presented in
this research.

The general topic will be what did the program managers find the most
challenging in their respective transitions?

Walt

Allocating: it was hard for him to leave the hands on approach of being
a technical specialist behind and finding his way to work through others,
was the most challenging for him. He remarked that he was frustrated by
the fact when he was trying to complete a task he wasn't able to do it himself. While he was a technical specialist he could work whatever hours it
took to get done…now no matter how many hours he works, it doesn't go
towards one project or task.

Dave

Abundance of issues: it was exhausting for him to juggle all the issues
going on and balancing those responsibilities. He commented on how he
now had to know accounting principals and contracts. He had trouble
knowing his boundaries mainly due to his getting in and dirty attitude and
his wanting to figure everything out.

Bill

Relationships: he had the most challenges with building personal relationships, the interactions and the dynamics of your once co-workers perceptions are after his transition into management.

Chris

Relationships: he had indicated that the dynamics of how you interact with the technical specialist, from being a peer to a manager. Chris had several remarks of his most challenging moments in the transitional phase. Another was his being able to work and manage things at the same time he spent long hours working and had a lot on his plate when it came to managing other things as well as it just wasn't one thing. He had enormous things going on and it was hard for him to find the focus he needed as well as being able to balance them. He indicated the third thing that was the most challenging was allocating the workload and getting the results he envisioned.

Joe

Abundance of issues: he realized that being in a manger's role involved a balancing of many more responsibilities, how to make priorities and assign tasks. He commented that his new role as manager was taking up all his time and that he wasn't able to complete some of the technical task that was asked of him. He clearly say's in his transition he is still being required to perform as a technical specialist and that he finds himself not being able to complete everything that is required with the new job title and aspect of that title.

Joe also says the constant interruptions and having to jump through hoops from one task to the other as he had to drop what he was doing in which he was at least half way done and go into something else. He further goes on by saying when he was a technical specialist he had days to figure out and solve a problem…now he longer has that luxury.

<u>Summation of the Five Interviewees</u>

The above statements by the interviewees show some of their most challenging issues in their transition. The following comment made by Dave is a succinct statement, which will help demonstrate the overall opinion about the transition and how rough it was:

- "I thought it would be much easier then what it really turned out to be...things were not made easy...it was the roughest thing I may have encountered in my life time...it was truly exhausting...the skill sets needed for a management role...the DIAWA certification process...I had no idea what I was getting myself into."

Table 2 will indicate what the interviewees found the most challenging and difficult in the transition.

Ranking of all the Interviewees

The results of the data collected by the interview were arranged in a manner that the researcher was able to depict some major areas of concerns and they were presented to the program managers for their ranking. The program managers would then rank then in the order that they felt was of importance to them based on their transition into the management competency within the federal government of the department of defense. The results of such will found in the table 2 on the following page.

Table 2
Areas of discussion as per survey questions

Question	Rank the difficulty				
	Walt	Dave	Bill	Chris	Joe
1. Abundance of issues: the programs manager As balancing more responsibilities and task ECT.	3	1	2	1	1
2. Staffing: manpower getting the work accomplished, finding time and help for others	5	2	5	4	5
3. New guy on the block: a TS to a PM a lot of learning	6	3	6	5	6
4. Affiliations: relationship, interactions and perceptions since the promotion to PM	2	5	1	2	2
5. Allocating: giving up the hands on and getting things done through others	2	5	1	2	2
6. Expectations: what was assumed by management and how your perceptions were and were skill sets needed	4	4	4	6	4

Conclusion of Chapter 4

As this researcher concluded this chapter and analyzed the answers to the survey questions posed along with the snap shot of table 2 as how the program managers ranked the issues of importance as it related to them. It showed that the transition was very difficult the skill sets that they had wasn't sufficient enough to handle a managerial function.

The transition wasn't as smooth as it could have been with a little more planning and skill sets acquired and the possibilities of mentoring would have made a great difference. The reluctance of help by upper management.

In chapter 5 of this research this writer will summarize and conclude and make recommendations as it relates to technical specialist transitioning into the management competency.

Chapter 5
Summary, Discussion and Recommendations

Summary

The purpose of this study was to explore the challenges that were faced by technical specialist in their transition into a management competency within the department of defense branch of the federal government.

Furthermore, it was to grasp a better understanding of the uphill challenges faced in their transition through their own experiences and what skill sets they thought they lacked. In addition, to just the skills required in the newly appointed program managers had to complete the DIAWA certification process.

The program mangers indicated via phone calls that it took them an average of three years to become comfortable with their positions. They also indicated if they knew what was truly expected of them they would have better prepared for their transition. Much managerial type of skills was required that the technical specialist did not possess.

As this researcher reviewed literature on similar transitions in the private sector was difficult as well (a few examples with Aucoin, 2002; Badawy, 1995; Gray, 1979; and Hill, 2003). Regardless of the difficulty of the transition very little research has been done in this field and especially when it comes to governmental type of technical transitions into management ones.

Thereby, allowing a need for a research exploration of technical specialist found to be of significant issues from a technical specialist to manager were warranted. This study focused on the challenges and experiences of technical specialist encountered at a personal level of the transition. From this very selective group data the only five formal technical specialists to ever make the transition into the management competency even though they were at three different locations comprised collection.

This study started with an exploratory probing if the research would be of value to the organization and within the technical specialist group. By using a qualitative technique to rank the most important areas of discussion and issues to be formulated in a way to understand them in order of the most difficult or the most challenging. This rare occurrence was taken in the considerations of transitions of technical specialist into a management career field.

One of the limitations to this type of method was the locations; due to the fact basically there was only one or two of the managers at these locations. Furthermore, these results generally speaking are not with the general public. So the methodology that was chosen may have had a limited impact on a much wider research group.

As interviews were conducted with five former interviewees a descriptive survey was formulated to ask the most relative issues that technical specialist had in such a transition. The interview was to take no longer then 60 minutes and was transcribed once received by this researcher. The questioner provided the major data for this research. These managers were selected because they were the only technical specialists ever to make such a transition.

As the results of the interviews the data that was provided told a telling story about the transition from a technical competency to a management competency directly from the questions posed. The areas of discussion included: technical expertise related to managerial context during the transition; was the managerial more challenging then first thought; was a training developmental program available to assist in the new role; if there were certifications required for their new position and if so what was that like; what did they like and dislike about both; were there any organizational resources do they rely on and was there any commonality; what comments were made and seemed to be the main issues in the transition. The managers were asked about their likes and dislikes. What did they find to be the most challenging to overcome in the transition; there were 160 responses to the main subject matter as it related to the survey questioner. After receiving the results this researcher presented them to the managers and this writer formulated a ranking table for them to rank what they felt was of the most important issues.

The interviews were shown in chapter 4. The following will be the findings of the results.

Findings of the Research

This study was an eye opening experience and needed to be done. The very findings alone on the merit of the research showed many of the challenges and the difficulties involved in the transition.

It showed a major awareness that alarmed this researcher in that managers whom were already seasoned in the competency of management field and had completed the DIAWA certification process within the department of defense branch were not willing to help the newly appointed manager into the management competency field.

After such research was completed and after much review of the literature and after the comprising the data within the research resulted by the information collected via a descriptive survey questioner and it was no surprise to this researcher about what the certain skill sets would be needed to have the ability to make a transition into the management competency a much easier and smoother one.

An underling issues was the fact if better preparation was performed by the technical specialist and with management cooperation showing a type of interest in the technical specialist this could have and would have been a much more pleasant transition.

This could have easily been accomplished by allowing technical specialist the ability to have insight on what the expectations would be in the new position. And what skill sets would be needed and required for a position of such magnitude. This would have enabled a smoother transition and if once the prospected transitionee's totally understood this requirement the effort would have surely been put forth.

Furthermore, if upper management was more committed to helping technical specialist to getting promoted and looking at them as an asset rather then a burden their field may be able to benefit as well only if they the management would help.

Technical specialist could make the decision on if the management competency was right for them. As the research showed the technical specialist had problems significant challenges in the following skills:

- Communication
- Allocating
- Performance appraisals
- Relationships
- Pressures and stress
- Managing conflicts
- Motivating it subordinates

It was obvious from the survey it wasn't what they initially thought it was. It ended up being much tougher with extreme hours spent at work not being able to relinquish the hands on approach; they all battled with many of similar issues.

The program managers had allocating issues, since being a program manager how challenging it was to leave the hands on approach and getting task accomplished through others.

An abundance of issues as now being a program manager their roles had increase enormously, with such things as tasking and the setting of priorities more so then being a technical specialist.

Expectations of the new position and the perception they had of what it entailed of the newly appointed position. What the harsh reality truly was with the position.

How the affiliations with personal and mangers alike effected their perception and what took place within the work place. How their workforce changed towards them once the transition was completed.

Since becoming a program manager how the personal relationships changed and how the perceptions of the technical specialist changed towards them.

Discussion

In this section the discussion will entail what the commonalities were with the technical specialist and their transition into a program manager role. And use Hill's (2003); study for a comparison of a governmental study and a private sector study with similar issues.

Through the experiences that the program managers indicated by their responses in chapter 4 about their transition from a technical specialist lead to an invaluable insight into the very essences of the transition were discovered. The program managers were aware and concerned with the challenges of the transition and by such only the most memorable issues would be recorded.

This researcher recorded that the program manager's similarities were:

- Working longer hours
- Found a lack of mentoring
- Allocating task a mind set that was working through others to complete a task, rather then doing it themselves
- The many roles or hats they wore they could no longer focus on just one task any longer it was now multiple task
- The increase of pressure and stress as it related to the new responsibilities of being the program manger
- The need for better relationship skills, better know as people skills
- The need for training and insight of the position
- They always seemed to have issues with not enough resources
- Feeling as a novice due to the fact there's a lot to learn
- Feeling as now they were not perceived as one of the guys
- They all seemed to miss the hands-on approach and that was hard to over come

- A greater appreciation for their new roles as with it came with a much bigger picture of the total organizational goals and with such came an increase in the decision making process

- Motivating their work force

- Learning how to balance and prioritize tasks and the continuous interruptions throughout the day

- The urgency to drop what you are doing and go to something else no matter where you were in the other task which could be nearly completed or not

- Always seemed to be attending meaningless meetings

- The jealousy and the feeling of resentment by your fellow technical specialist once you move ahead of them

The above were issues in addition to the four main areas of the discussion that came out. The following were the four main issues of the transition:

- Abundance of issues

- Allocating

- Expectations of the new position

- Affiliation changes

In addition, to the above other areas came out such as being the new guy on the block. The need to develop new skill sets for management functions.

As this researcher studied the survey other issues such as stress and pressure emerged and were relevant to all program managers that took the survey. This also seemed to go hand and hand with the abundance of issues going on.

Relationships appeared to work regardless of not having enough resources to accomplish a task. This surely adds to the stress factor as far as this researcher is concerned.

It was also clear that being a new guy required new skill sets, which could have been accomplished if training was available. This would have made technical specialist better equip for the transition would have enabled a better understanding. Relationships between issues were important in giving recommendations of this research.

However, it was of great importance to have independent opinions as a perspective to be better understood. It was of this researcher's conclusion that the transition was truly a difficult one as discovered in the descriptive survey questioner this was support by the answers that were recorded. It was also noted that it was much different then first thought by the interviewees as presented within chapter 4.

Another surprising element of the transition was the relationship changes with their formal technical specialist they though things would be the same but now they were not considered one of them, and adversary, an enemy.

This researcher also found that through the survey that the average time for the technical specialist that transitioned into program management did not feel at ease with their position until 3 years. As the interviewees indicated:

- Walt with indicating 3 years

- Dave with indicating 2 years

- Bill with indicating 4 years

- Chris with indicating 3 years

- Joe with indicating 2.5 years

Similar Research Issues in the Private Sector

As discussed in earlier chapters Hill (2003) while conducting her study showed the her research was just as inadequate when it was in the technologist transitioning to management as she said: "despite its ubiquity and importance we know surprisingly little about the transition to management" (Hill, 2003. p.2) Furthermore, after her studies had been done on such transitions of how little we knew about what and how managers did their jobs" (p. 337).

This researcher agrees with her findings as this writer began analyzing the data it left more questions to be answered on other matters that arose from such a survey. Hill (2003) also noted the difficulty in the transition for a technologist into a management position was quite challenging as well. As this study showed technical specialist had many uphill challenges and the additional burden of completing the DIAWA certification process.

Latack, (1984) offered this insight:

> First, career transitions as a process, rather than an event, are relatively unexplored...it may be premature to base model building of career transitions on pre-existing theory...further studies might adopt a more exploratory, hypothesis generating approach aimed at describing and classifying how individuals react to different types of transitions, and what individual and organizational factors contribute to and alleviate stress during the transition. (p.317).

This researcher concurs with that statement because a survey of this magnitude can have a major effect on the stress levels obtained by even the though of contemplating such a move into management.

Hill (2003) made this statement "If management development initiatives are truly address the needs of new managers, they must be based on an underlining issues of how new managers think and feel about the experiences of becoming a manager. And this is why this writer chose her method of study as the same issues arose in her study and in these researchers as well. As these issues are bought to light a better understanding on the transition and the challenges faced by the technical specialist.

Hills (2003) objective was to describe the experiences of becoming a manager from a new manager's point of view. As this researcher wants to know as well Hill (2003) stated she "interviewed the new managers by phone" (p.339). Her studies incorporated phone interviews and she created a descriptive survey and due to the exploratory nature of this research a qualitative study will be devised to account for the main issues for technical advisors transitioning into the management competency.

One of the most noteworthy findings by large was stated by Hill (2003), which said, "Listening to them, it becomes clear that the transition to manager is not limited to acquiring competencies and buildings relationships. Rather, it constitutes a profound transformation, as individuals learn to think, feel, and value as managers" (Hill, 2003, p.5).

As one of the issues in this study was that the interviewees did not feel they were respected and they thought they were not skilled enough to perform the appointment. Hills (2003), studies indicated similar issues as well they were as follows:

- Managing effective relationships
- Expectations of the new position
- Roles, tasks, and delegating
- The feeling of being overwhelmed
- Many issues going on at one time
- Having to getting work done through others
- Communications
- Performance
- Stress and pressures of the new position
- Extended working hours
- New skill sets needed

As Hills (2003) study showed very much the same results of this researchers study with many of the similarities and issues being the same.

Recommendations

Based on these researchers' studies the need for future research is necessary, further research should to make a much wider survey that includes a broader pool of contributors and to see if other governmental agencies need to be highlighted as well. It was of great concern by this researcher that once the technical specialist was promoted into the management competency the seasoned managers did not offer help or any mentorship to those newly appointed managers.

This researcher asks why this is like it is. Maybe because the technical specialist is still considered a technical type expert and not held in the highest regard and of having a true management background. And if this is the case how are the technical specialist viewed as they do become more settled in their new position.

This research came to no surprise by this writer who realized that more skill sets would be required and by the interviewees answers confirmed it. It is clearly indicated that technical specialist need to be better prepared for the transition and they should be told what is expected from them and what skill sets would be of most benefit. These skills include the following:

- People skills
- Communications skills
- Delegating skills
- Motivation skills
- Performance appraisal skills
- Managing conflicts
- Stress
- Relationships skills
- Administrative skill as to functions the business end of things
- Balancing and prioritization skills

This researcher strongly suggests that if any technical specialist is considering such a career move that they research what is required to perform that new role and to understand the challenges they may face and the uphill struggles they may encountered. Once they decide to do so ask for some guidance and get some training in some of the skill sets that were mentioned above.

This researcher believes if the proper training was completed on the initial phase of their transition a much smoother and less frustrating issues could be arise.

Technical specialists who are considering such should not view asking for help as a weakness. This writer can just about guarantee that they would regret it. If they were offered the chance for help and did not capitalize on it.

This writer highly recommends that upper senior managers in the management competency understand how a technical specialist feels and what challenges that they face during their transition. To assign a mentor to prospected technical specialist and instill the skills needed in being a fully capable and successful manager.

This writer recommends that a training track be established for those who wish to become a manager even though it is out of the realm of their present position just because they are in another competency that isn't related to a manger field should not hinder their desires to better themselves.

In concluding this study and paper this writer can only hope it serves to help those who desire the challenges faced in the transition in to management. It is the intention of this writer to shed some light on the issues faced by technical specialist trying to expand their growth potential with in the department of defense in the federal government.

References

Aucoin, B. Michael (2002). <u>From Engineer to Manager</u>: mastering the transition. Norwood, MA: Artech House Inc.

Badawy, M. K. (1995). <u>Developing managerial skills in engineers and scientists (2nd ed.).</u> New York: John Wiley & Sons, Inc.

Belker, L. B. (1997). <u>The First Time Manager (4th ed.)</u> New York, N.Y. AMACOM

Buhler, P. (2001). <u>Management Skills in 24 Hours</u>. Indianapolis, IN. Alpha Books.

Carroll, A. B. (1987). <u>In Search of the Moral Manager</u>. Business Horizons, March/April 1987, pp 7-15.

Certo S. C. (1997). <u>Modern Management: Diversity, Quality, Ethics, and the Global Environment (7th ed.)</u> Upper Saddle River, N.J. Prentice Hall

Cooper, D. & Schindler, P. (2003). <u>Business Research Methods (8th ed.).</u> New York, NY. McGraw-Hill Companies, Inc.

Creswell, J.W. (1998). <u>Qualitative Inquiry and Research Design</u>: Choosing Among Five Traditions. Thousand Oaks, Ca. Sage.

Donnelly, J., Gibson, J. & Ivancevich, J. (1981). <u>Fundamentals of Management: Functions, Behavior, Models (4th ed.).</u> Plano, TX. Business Publications, Inc.

Druker, P. (2003). <u>On the Profession of Management</u>. Boston. MA. Harvard Business Review

Gray, I. (1979), The Engineer In Transition to Management. New York, NY. IEEE Press: John Wiley & Sons, Inc

Hill, L. A. (2003). Becoming a manager: How New Managers Master the Challenges of Leadership. Boston MA: Harvard Business School Publishing Corporation.

Latack, J.C. (1984). "Career Transitions within organizations: An Exploratory study of work, nonwork, and coping strategies. "Organizational Behavior & Human Performance, 34,296-322

Lincoln Y., & Guba, E. (1985). Naturalistic inquiry. Beverly Hills, CA: Sage.

Maister, D. H. (1993). Managing The Professional Service Firm. New York, NY: Free Press Paperbacks.

Maslow, A. H. (1998). Maslow On Management. New York, NY. : John Wiley & Sons, Inc.

Meredith, J.R., & Mantel S. J. (2000). Project Management: A managerial Approach, (4th ed.). New York, NY. : John Wiley & Sons, Inc.

Maxwell, J. A. (1996). Qualitative research design: An interactive approach. Thousand Oaks, CA: Sage Publications, Inc.

McCracken, G. (1988). The long interview. Newbury Park, CA: Sage.

Mavroules, N. (1991). Creating a professional acquisition workforce. National Contract Management Journal, 24 (2), pp. 15-23.

Mintzberg. H. (2004). Managers not MBAs. San Francisco, Ca: Berrett-Koehler Publishers, Inc.

Montana P. J. & Charnov B. H. (2000). Management (3rd ed.) Hauppauge, NY: Barron's Educational Series, Inc.

Moustakas, C. (1994). Phenomenological Research Methods. Thousand Oaks, Ca. Sage

President's Blue Ribbon Commission on Defense Management. (1986). Report of the President's Blue Ribbon Commission on Defense Management. Washington, D.C.: Government Printing Office.

Thamhain, Han J. "<u>Developing the skills you need</u>", Research Technology Management, March/April 1992, p.42

Yin, R. K. (1994). <u>Case study research: Design and methods</u>. Thousand Oaks, CA: Sage.

Appendix A

Transitioning from a Technical Competency to a Management
Competency within the Department of Defense branch of the Federal
Government

Cover Letter

Martin K. Younts

June 10, 2004

Dear Sir:

I am currently pursuing a Ph.D. in Engineering Management. My dissertation relates to the above topic of transitioning from a technical competency to a management competency as technical specialist appoints are rare and you being one of those who had successfully made the transition I wish to conduct an interview as it relates to that topic.

My reason in contacting you as I stated above is that you are one of five who have successfully made the transitions from being a former technical specialist so I ask for your participation by filling out and completing the questioner survey interview form that is enclosed. The information you provide will be summarized only within the dissertation. And was comprised will be shared with the other four so that a ranking of issues can be addressed and then can help further technical specialist in trying to make the transition.

I have included six questions that I think will cover the transition that were faced by the technical specialist on the interview form. Your responses would be appreciated and my desire is to receive them by email, which you have and can find on the global address book. Once received, it will be extracted and placed in an interviewee folder. The email will then be deleted. If you feel uncomfortable responding by email please reply by hard copy or please feel free to call me as we have spoke on this matter early on the inception of this project.

Thank you for your time and cooperation in this study.

Sincerely,

Martin K. Younts

Interview/Consent Form

Technical Specialist face a challenging transition in the attempt to move into the management field. Please fill out the following interview relative to your experiences with what your transition experience was like into the management competency. By filling this form out you are also consenting in the participation of this survey.

PRELIMINARY INFORMATION

Name: _____

Location of position: _____

Years with the government: _____

Years as a Technical Specialist: _____

Years you felt comfortable with your management appointment: _____

1. How was your technical expertise related to a managerial related context during the transition from TS to a PM. (TS means Technical Specialist, PM means Program Manager)?

2. Were the management aspects of the position more challenging then first thought, and once appointed to management was there a career development program?

3. Were there and certifications needed to be completed and if so what was the process like?

4. What was your likes about being a TS and now as a PM, and the same for your dislikes on both of the positions?

5. How did if any individual and organizational resources did they rely on and were there any commonalities between being a technical specialist and a program manager?

6. How difficult was and what were your main issues in the transition from TS to PM?

Signature of the interviewee: _____
By signing and furnishing this information you are herby consenting to this study.

Interview tracking number: _____

Ranking Form

Please rank the following 1–6 with a numeric grade, one being the highest ranking of difficulty and 6 being the least in difficulty

<u>Rank the difficulty</u>

Question

---

1. Abundance of issues: the programs manager
    as balancing more responsibilities and task ect.   _____

2. Staffing: manpower getting the work
    accomplished, finding time and help for others   _____

3. New guy on the block: TS to a PM a lot of
    learning   _____

4. Affiliations: relationship, interactions and
    perceptions since the promotion to PM   _____

5. Allocating: giving up the hands on and
    getting things done through others   _____

6. Expectations: what was assumed by
    management and how your perceptions were
    and were skill sets needed   _____

About the Author

Martin K. Younts has consulted coast-to-coast. He is a member of the American Management Association (AMA), American Society of Quality (ASQ) and the Acquisition Workforce Society (AWS) In Addition to his membership affiliations he holds certifications in *General Management, Quality Improvement Management, Manufacturing Management* and *Strategic Leadership*. He holds a Bachelors of Science in Engineering Technology (B.S.E.T), a Masters of Science in Engineering Management (M.S.E.M) and Masters of Business Administration (M.B.A).

He has worked in several areas through out his 30 plus year career. He has guided companies through their re-engineering processes, has helped identify and resolved company issues such as marketing, absenteeism, material waste due to lack of training. He has improved quality by implementing Six Sigma, Lean and Fusion Management concepts and mythologies. He has instilled proven Time Management skill sets so organizations operate in an effective and efficient manner. These are just a few processes that he has provided to American companies today.

Mr. Younts is currently completing his Doctorates in Engineering Management once completed he plans to write a book on the Complexities of American Business in the new Era of Leadership, in this he lays out his new innovative methods of what he calls L.I.M.E's Methods which stands for *Leadership, Integrity, Morals* and *Ethics*. Mr. Younts believes these are the basic *core values* that are lacking in American Business today.

He enjoys helping others in understanding what it takes to succeed in *management*.

If you would like to learn more or receive additional information on Mr. Younts proven methods please visit: www.firstadvantageconsultingfirm.com or call 866-842-0187

978-0-595-39594-1
0-595-39594-5

www.ingramcontent.com/pod-product-compliance
Lightning Source LLC
Chambersburg PA
CBHW021544200526
45163CB00015B/1196